Birds of Town and Village

Birds of Town and Village

PAINTINGS BY BASIL EDE

Text by W. D. Campbell *from W. D. Campbell, Christmas 1982*

Foreword by H.R.H. The Prince Philip,
Duke of Edinburgh

COUNTRY LIFE BOOKS

Published by Country Life Books
and distributed for them by
The Hamlyn Publishing Group Limited
London · New York · Sydney · Toronto
Astronaut House, Feltham, Middlesex, England

First published 1965
Tenth impression 1979

ISBN 0 600 43021 9

Printed in England by
Balding & Mansell, Wisbech

Foreword

By H.R.H. The Prince Philip, Duke of Edinburgh

I find books about birds almost impossible to resist. The combination of an entertaining and informative text with the excellent reproductions of the artist's extremely accurate and attractive pictures makes this book quite irresistible.

Watching, recognising and listening to birds adds a whole new dimension to the enjoyment of life, and this book, which concentrates on the birds most likely to be seen and heard near houses, should be a most useful starting point for many people as yet only vaguely aware of the grace and beauty of birds.

Contents

Introduction

Recently, in a press review of an excellent new book on British birds, the critic (himself a knowledgeable amateur ornithologist) expressed the conviction that the time for such hand-illustrated productions had now passed; in his view, photography, and particularly high-speed colour photography, could now reveal the absolute truth as to the appearance of a live bird, whereas the bird-artist, however skilful, could only portray his impression of the subject. To me this is an unacceptable opinion; the main achievement of modern lenses and high-speed shutters has been to reveal what the human eye cannot detect. A 'still' of a humming-bird in action is technically fascinating, but is nevertheless a representation of a static pose which had no real separate existence; and even the same wing-action, captured by a ciné-camera, is only of value when artificially slowed down. To the observer, even though, thanks to such modern aids, he may understand the mechanics of the wing-movement, the humming-bird in action will still give the impression of a clearly visible body suspended between two vibrating blurs. Thus the artist has the advantage over the camera in that he records a subject as seen by a human eye—and this applies to colour as well as to form.

Another criticism frequently heard with regard to paintings of birds is that the artist portrays his subjects in a state of perfection rarely seen in the field. There is some truth underlying this complaint: not all birds seen are adults in their best breeding plumage—indeed, when any species is at its most plentiful, immediately after the breeding season, the duller juveniles are bound to be those most frequently met with; and the human eye cannot take in much detail except of comparatively still objects at close quarters. But the point which I must stress is that birds *can* be seen in the full beauty of colour, form and surface-texture such as is displayed in this book. There are many and varied aids towards achieving such ideal visions, of which some of the most helpful are patience, inquisitiveness, binoculars, bird-tables—and luck.

This, then, is one of the main objects of this book—to depict a sample of the varied and beautiful bird-life available within reach of our dwellings, as seen by a sensitive eye and recorded by a gifted hand.

The choice of species may to some seem arbitrary, and indeed many factors, varying from geographical location of the town or village to the status of a species at one particular point in time, may influence one's conception of commonness or rarity. Many of the species chosen tend to be less plentiful in northern Britain, but the converse is also true, as, for example, in the case of the grey wagtail. It so happens that this book was conceived just as the effects of the catastrophic winter of 1962–3 were becoming apparent, and doubts were felt as to whether kingfishers, goldcrests, grey wagtails, and even the once ubiquitous wren, could be classed as reasonably common birds; but faith in their powers of resurgence seems to have been justified. In a few years' time, it now seems safe to prophesy, at least one other species will have to be included in a selection such as this, for our latest acquisition, the collared dove, has now succeeded in colonising Britain almost literally from Land's End to John o' Groats, and is increasing in numbers annually—and always near human habitations. Other species may occur or disappear as a direct result of human activities; thus sand martins may be temporarily common when local gravel-digging affords good nesting-sites, but are forced to seek new quarters when the disused pits are filled with municipal (or Rural District) refuse. Of the fifty-six birds depicted, all except one (the mallard) are included in a total of seventy species which have been seen at least once within (as opposed to flying over) my own garden. In my present location, where I have been for sixteen years, exactly thirty of the total are regular annual visitors or residents, and an average of any five of the remainder is also recorded each year. Merely by extending the range by a hundred yards (thus including a brook, meadows, hedges and a small pond) no fewer than a further thirty species have been observed, thus bringing the list of almost backdoor birds to be seen in a country village to just one hundred. A further mile and a half, to take in both downland and the river, would add at least another sixteen birds which might possibly be seen, still well within the parish.

Another aim of this work, apart from the purely æsthetic appeal of the illustrations, is that the pictures and text together may form a reference book which will not only lead to the identification of some of our commonest birds, but also stimulate interest in their habits and behaviour. Another more subtle intention is that once these basic fifty-six species are thoroughly known, the observer will become so interested that he or she will desire to name any of the three hundred or so other species which may be encountered in Britain.

Fears are often expressed as to the future of birds, as more and more land is used up for housing and roads, and as more and more field hedges are being eradicated to form larger units more suitable for mechanised farming. But birds are on the whole very adaptable creatures, and many of the haunts which we tend to think of as 'natural' for certain species—buildings for swallows, house martins, swifts and house sparrows; gardens for robins, blackbirds, song thrushes and dunnocks; ploughed fields for rooks, lapwings and starlings—are themselves artificial substitutes for some primitive habitat. Even the roofs of the skyscrapers in American cities have proved acceptable both to ground-nesting and cliff-haunting species of birds. A far greater danger, now established beyond all doubt, is that arising from the use of almost indestructible poisons, mainly insecticides, in farming and gardening. Some progress has already been made to lessen this threat, but it may be that this has come too late to save our birds of prey. Just as it has been suggested that the collared dove would have to be included in a list of common birds of town and village in a very few years' time, it now seems almost as certain that even the commonest of hawks, the kestrel, will by then no longer be eligible for inclusion.

As readers of the text will doubtless gather, a great deal of first-hand information about birds can be obtained while the observer is usefully employed in his garden. It seems that most species have little fear of steady, rhythmical movement, such as that of digging, hoeing, or thinning and weeding. In addition to observations on food, aggressive behaviour, gathering of nesting-materials, and actual breeding activities (all helping to supply answers to the question 'What is this bird doing in my garden?'), the basis of some of the apparently dogmatic assertions as to food-preferences of different species is founded on more precise experimental evidence—that of actually catching birds (very temporarily) in cages baited with varying natural foods. Thus if a battery of about a score of cage-traps, alternately baited with aphids and red-currants, is placed among the peas when warblers are on the move in late July, and as a result chiffchaffs are caught in the aphis traps, willow warblers and white-throats equally distributed among the aphis traps and the currant traps, and blackcaps and lesser whitethroats almost entirely in the currant traps, one can, after many seasons of such investigations, reach a pretty definite conclusion—but only, it should be stressed, as to feeding preference when a choice is available at one particular time of the year.

A fitting ending to this section (and an encouragement to late beginners in the fascinating study of birds) is that about thirty-five years ago (when I was in my middle twenties) a letter appeared in *Country Life* asking any readers who were at all interested in birds to send in records to a county ornithological society. Although at that time I was far more interested in butterflies, moths and wild flowers, the sight of a new bird—a grey wagtail—on the manure-heap in the garden caused me to send in my first record. Since then I have watched birds in many places from the Camargue to Lapland; but nevertheless about ninety per cent of my most fruitful bird-watching has taken place in or around country villages.

W.D.C.

Cholsey, Berkshire.

The Rook and the Carrion Crow

The Rook On account of its numbers, its gregariousness, and its inclination to co-exist with man, the rook should be the best-known of the four black crows which occur in Britain; it should therefore be the most worthy of a distinctive and unambiguous name. Yet this neighbourly bird has often to share the name 'crow' with the next species. This failure to differentiate between two species which are very similar in general appearance, but quite distinct in habits, is apparently of long standing. The proverbial 'as the crow flies' must surely refer to the familiar flight-lines of rooks to and from their rookeries or winter roosts; Shakespeare leaves no doubt as to the bird he had in mind when 'light thickens, and the crow makes wing to the rooky wood', and even Tennyson, with his 'many-wintered crow that leads the clanging rookery home', seems to have considered the names as permissible alternatives.

The outstanding characteristic of the rook is its sociability throughout the whole year. A rookery is probably the most familiar example of colonial breeding, so much so that the term has been borrowed for breeding assemblies of penguins and even seals. But even more impressive than the busy nesting communities are the winter roosting assemblies, when a central rookery becomes the nightly gathering-place for rooks within a radius of some five or six miles. The same routine as that of starlings is followed; small parties or long straggling streams converge toward the 'rooky wood', but are in no hurry to enter. They gather noisily on tall trees at some distance from their destination, and here seem to await a full muster from all directions before making the next move. By this time some five or six thousand rooks, often accompanied by about half as many jackdaws, may have gathered. Suddenly, as if at a signal from some unseen conductor's baton, the cawing and yapping ceases, and the whole mass, silent except for the rush of wings, swoops down to assemble on the ground. Here, for some minutes, they feed, or at least go through the ritual of walking over the ground as if in search of food. The final flight into the roost is just as sudden and concerted as the preliminary descent to the ground, but the temporary hush is now broken. Voices and wingbeats unite to form a Niagara-like background of noise, in which individual caws and yelps can still be heard.

The rook's status in farm economy is controversial. It certainly does take some seed corn, but it also eats tremendous quantities of corn pests, such as wireworms. The grain consumed at harvest, although a staple article of diet at this season, is of little importance—it is almost entirely gleaned from the ground and therefore would not have been garnered in any case. Corn production and rooks can and do thrive side by side.

The Carrion Crow This bird closely resembles the rook in size, colour and proportions, and there the similarity ends, for the carrion crow is an individualistic freebooter rather than a mass-conforming commuter. Outside the breeding season foraging parties of a score or so, or even more than a hundred, may be attracted to feed together at worthwhile sites such as refuse-dumps or muddy foreshores, but during the breeding season a pair nesting in isolation is the usual rule. Being a much more adaptable bird than its sociable cousin, the crow, although often sharing typical rook country, can also find both nesting sites and sustenance in less artificial habitats—craggy mountains, bleak moorland or coastal cliffs. Unlike the rook, it will forage among scrub or rank vegetation.

Notes on The Rook

HAUNTS Restricted by very specialised feeding and nesting requirements—needs extensive open ground, with short vegetation and preferably with exposed soil, for feeding, and tall trees (but not dense woodland) for nesting. Farming therefore provides ideal conditions, and throughout Britain rook is almost entirely a hanger-on of agricultural man.

APPEARANCE Apart from carrion crow the only common large all-black British land-bird. Distinguishable from former by: (i) Communal nesting and feeding habits; (ii) Bare whitish skin on face and throat; but note that this does not apply to juveniles and first-winter birds, whose faces are as black-feathered as crows; (iii) Beak appears more tapered and somewhat longer than that of crow; (iv) Somewhat shaggier plumage, particularly noticeable in 'baggy-kneed' effect produced by loose plumage around leg; (v) Purplish-blue, rather than greenish-blue, gloss on plumage; (vi) More rapid wing-beat in flight.

VOICE Well-known mellow caw in contrast with harsher note of crow; also much wider vocal range than latter, including high-pitched falsetto call.

FOOD Omnivorous—earthworms, insect larvae, snails, corn, peas, potatoes, acorns; food mainly taken from ground, largely found by digging and probing. Trees visited for food mainly during rearing of young, when caterpillar-infested oaks are favourite source of supply; walnuts and acorns may also be plucked direct from trees. Will occasionally resort to more crow-like diet—carrion, eggs, and small birds or mammals.

NESTING Usually in uppermost twigs of tall trees, particularly deciduous species such as elm, beech and oak, but not infrequently in conifers. Nest massive structure of twigs, growing with age, since old nest may be added to year after year. Live twigs gathered for building. Mud, turf or dung used to consolidate mass, and deep cup formed of hay, straw, moss and sometimes wool. 4–6 eggs, usually greenish, heavily mottled with brown.

Notes on The Carrion Crow

HAUNTS No marked preference for any one type of country. Although quite at home in treeless moorland or barren coastal areas, flat or rocky, birds in suitable areas, unlike rook, may inhabit dense woodland, provided that some open patches are available.

APPEARANCE About same size as rook; main differences listed under that species.

VOICE Usual call a deep, harsh 'kraah', sometimes with a slight gurgling effect. Near nest will indulge in distinct song, often from low perch such as hedge or gatepost. This, a harsh guttural rattle, has little carrying power.

FOOD Like rook, omnivorous, but with a distinct bias towards flesh, whether insect, bird, reptile, mollusc, fish or mammal. Carrion feeder on larger corpses, as of sheep, but direct predator on smaller animals—mice, eggs and young birds, young rabbits. Will often prey on injured quarry much larger than itself, usually with mate or with more numerous accomplices.

NESTING In trees often much lower than rook, and often in a crutch or fork rather than in twigs; in treeless areas low bushes or rock-ledges. Nest basically like that of rook, but usually more compact, and materials of main structure varying with surroundings. Cup well-lined with wool or similar soft material. Clutch of up to 5 eggs, very like those of rook, but slightly rounder.

1.. Rook (above). Carrion Crow (below)

The Jackdaw

Like the rook, the jackdaw is sociable all the year round; but unlike the rook it is sufficiently distinct in both size and plumage to escape confusion with any other crow, and therefore is not only generally well known by name, but the name itself now carries the seal of human recognition—a Christian name prefix. The 'Jack' here may not be entirely a term of endearment in the same class as Robin and Jenny for some smaller favourites, since it is a reasonable interpretation of the bird's common call, but even if it is not a sign of downright affection, it at least carries a hint of admiration, like that enjoyed by a likeable rogue. Although a frequent hanger-on of the rook in areas which happen to suit both species, the jackdaw can live in independent communities where its tree-tied cousin can find no foothold. Like the carrion crow, it can flourish in treeless areas among crags or cliffs, but unlike that species it has readily taken to artificial surroundings as well, and has become an established town-dweller. This arises not from any special adaptability which the other crows lack, but from the fact that it is a hole-nester, whether in hollow trees or rock-crevices, and man-made structures provide a diversity of suitable dark cavities, from the humble chimney-pot for one pair to the church-steeple which may house a colony.

Jackdaws are highly skilled fliers, and in fine weather spend a great deal of time in what can only be considered as aerial play, often ascending in soaring parties to a great height, and then tumbling towards earth in nose-dives, zig-zags and spirals. Even in sedate parties of rooks earnestly winging their way towards a winter-roost the accompanying jackdaws are very prone to indulge in minor spells of aerobatics to enliven the solemn procession. The jackdaw does not seem to need the wide feeding-range of the rook, and is content to scavenge in comparatively small areas, whether on coastal mud or rocks, town rubbish-dumps, allotments, or waste-ground, or even in a city park; but lately it has shown further signs of extending its scavenging activities to keep up with the times; the litter scattered around the receptacles provided for it at lay-bys on busy roads is not always due to human slovenliness —the early morning motorist may catch sight of the jackdaw culprits in the act of rifling the contents in search of edible scraps.

Although such readiness to exploit a new situation, combined with a wise grey eye and a jaunty confident walk, all suggest a highly intelligent bird, in one aspect of its nest-building the jackdaw displays either extreme stupidity or supreme optimism. When faced with a natural vertical cavity or a chimney, the technique for laying a foundation is to drop long sticks in until one lodges crossways. The daily accumulation in a hearth below a still clear chimney tells its own story of wasted time and materials; but the extreme example of this hopeless perseverance came from jackdaws which continually dropped 'starting-sticks' through some slits near the top of a very tall church steeple. All dropped straight to the belfry a hundred feet below, and although two cart-loads accumulated in four years, all was labour in vain.

Notes on The Jackdaw

HAUNTS Almost anywhere, town or country, inland or sea-side, provided that requisite nesting-sites and foraging areas are available.

APPEARANCE Much smaller size, and conspicuous grey on nape and sides of face, distinguish it from larger and all-black rook and carrion crow; young slightly browner, and with very striking china-blue eye—latter becomes pale grey in adult.

VOICE A noisy bird, both in flight and at rest; normal call a sharp 'chack'; in excitement, such as communal aerial exercises, calls often run together to produce laughing 'chack-chack-chack-chack'.

FOOD A very wide range of both animal and vegetable matter—worms, grubs, beetles from grassland; mice, frogs, eggs and young of birds from foraging in denser vegetation; sometimes joins crows and magpies at large carrion (one carrion crow, two magpies and three jackdaws once seen to emerge from inside carcase of fallow deer), and will readily take dead mice thrown out from traps. Also one of few birds in Britain which shows any signs of being a parasite hunter on cattle—frequently seen probing in fleece on sheep. Vegetable food includes grain, acorns, fruit and small potatoes.

NESTING In hole of tree, rock, or building—usually not far removed from daylight. In favourable sites, such as large many-hollowed oak or poplar, or in accessible buildings, a distinctly colonial nester. Main structure is normally of sticks, often of considerable thickness, but amount varies with nature of hole; in horizontal hollow, sticks may be dispensed with, or mere token deposit made; large amount of soft lining material—wool, hair, fur, grass, rags or binder-twine. About 5 eggs, slightly greenish blue, spotted or blotched variably with brownish-black.

2. Jackdaw

The Magpie

The familiar sight of a magpie, busily engaged in breaking up and turning over dried 'cow-pats' in search of dung-beetle maggots, calls to mind Macbeth's reference to 'maggot-pies' (together with choughs and rooks as birds used in divination), and one might conclude that this must have been the original form of the name, bestowed on account of such feeding activities. But this is a false clue, for within living memory (and fittingly in Shakespeare's 'Cotsall' district) 'Maggot' was still in use as a playful variant of Margaret. As with the jackdaw, the bestowal of a Christian name is probably a mark of familiarity or notoriety rather than affection, and probably no other bird has been used so frequently as the type of so many human failings—from lightfingeredness, garrulousness and hoarding to a fondness for ostentatious apparel.

The conspicuous pied plumage, the long tail which seems almost an encumbrance in flight, the chattering voice and the habit of feeding well out in open fields, all combine to make this a species unlikely to be overlooked; but in this country (although the exact contrary is true of Scandinavia) although not shy, it is extremely wary and stealthy in the neighbourhood of man. Since it is an expert at discovering the nests of birds, both on the ground and in bushes or trees, and eats both eggs and young, doubtless its wariness is the result of generations of enmity between keepers and farmers and its kind, and in areas where there is no intensive game-preservation the magpie may be much more confident in human surroundings. Although its depredations among game-birds' eggs and chicks are undeniable, it could be a bird of some economic value if it were more plentiful and tolerated, for its chief 'vice' becomes a virtue when directed against the wood pigeon—the easily-found eggs of the latter, particularly from hedgerows, are as eagerly sought and consumed as those of pheasant and partridge.

In areas where it is plentiful the magpie exhibits the usual sociability common to most of the crow family, and once the breeding-season is over parties of anything from ten to thirty may frequently be seen together. The presence of such a party concentrated at one spot may be the indication of the presence of carrion, from a dead rabbit to a dead sheep; and almost certainly a magpie rising from the road at the approach of a vehicle will reveal the point at which some squashed traffic-victim—hedgehog, rabbit, rat or bird—is lying. The habit, when in small parties or flocks, of flying off in single file, often with considerable intervals between each bird, makes this a species which one automatically counts as one bird after another comes into view, and there are numerous versions of the good luck or ill fortune foretold by each number; perhaps this superstition is a relic of the belief which Macbeth had in the significance of the actions of his 'maggot-pie'.

Notes on The Magpie

HAUNTS Open country with some bushes and trees—grassland (particularly grazing-land) with tall hedges or near edges of thicker woodland, bushy commons with open ground, or even more barren country with few trees and bushes.

APPEARANCE Combination of black and white plumage and long tail, together with size (body about the same size as that of jackdaw) make identification easy. At rest white appears as patch on each wing and on lower underparts; remainder is glossy black, iridescent with green, purple and blue. In flight rather short wings (in which white, black-margined primaries are conspicuous) accentuated by disproportionate length of tail. Young are of similar pattern, but black is duller.

VOICE A succession of chattering notes, with harsh, guttural tone—'kak-kak-kak-kak'.

FOOD Except during breeding-season of other birds, mainly worms, insects and larvae from ground, augmented by carrion as available; eggs and young of many birds; vegetable matter includes grain, fruit, beechmast and acorns; latter two items often carried off and hoarded.

NESTING Position very variable—sometimes quite low in dense hedge or bush, but frequently as high as crown of mature elm. The most skilled builder among our crows, for in addition to typical base of sticks solidified with turf, dung or mud, lattice-work dome of thorny twigs, with side-opening, is built above; lining of fine roots, or occasionally grass-stems. 5–6 eggs, greenish-blue closely marked with brown and grey spots or mottlings.

22

3. Magpie

The Jay

This, the most colourful in plumage of all our crows, is also the one which least often allows its fine feathers to be seen to full advantage, for in addition to being extremely wary, it is more entirely confined to woodland than any other British member of its family. The commonest indications of its presence are the raucous alarm call, followed by a fleeting glimpse of the white rump as it disappears through thick foliage. But, as with the magpie, this distrust of man may be the result of persecution as a pest not only by the gamekeeper, but also by the gardener or fruit-grower. Certainly in areas where suburbia has reached out to the edge of woodland (as around Epping Forest) the jay may become a fearless garden visitor, even to the extent of coming to the bird-table. Since it has varied tastes in the matter of vegetable food, from fruit to peas and broad beans, and since, moreover, it does not merely eat its fill, but also stuffs its capacious throat-pouch before leaving, it could be a much more widespread garden pest but for one characteristic which limits its depredations—a distaste for crossing open country for even a few hundred yards. Thus the areas in which it can be the most regular nuisance are either those immediately bordering woodland, or those to which intervening bushes or hedges can serve as stepping-stones from and to the woods.

Jays frequently occur in small parties, but seldom in flocks unless some special food supply, such as acorns and, of course, orchards of apples or cherries, causes a local population to concentrate in one particular feeding-area. The very conspicuous white rump, in most species (house martin, wheatear, brambling, bullfinch and many waders) a sure indication that at some period of the year its members associate and travel in flocks, therefore seems a superfluous 'follow-my-leader' mark in the case of the jay; one should stress here 'British jay' for its continental counterpart does periodically have to undertake winter movements in food-seeking flocks. Jays are so seldom seen in high direct flight that at first (especially if the light catches the pale rump and dark tail) a party passing over at a few hundred feet up could be taken for fieldfares. Such chances of seeing this bird in an unfamiliar setting occur in the occasional autumns when notable influxes of continental birds of this species take place.

Although the jay, ably assisted by the blackbird, is one of the chief alarmists of the woods, during the breeding-season it exercises remarkable restraint, and usually slips away from its nest in complete silence at the approach of an intruder.

In one five-acre walled garden which was in a very vulnerable position—bordered by close woodland on two sides and wooded park on the other two—the jays were reputed to know both the time of the day and the days of the week, for they were immediately present the moment the gate clicked behind the last of the staff as they trooped off to breakfast, lunch or home—and, of course, just as quickly absent when the human movement was in the reverse direction. The only explanation which seems to account for the punctual arrival on such occasions is that somewhere from a vantage point in the surrounding trees at least one patient jay was continually on watch, ready to give the 'all clear' at the appropriate moment.

Notes on The Jay

HAUNTS Woodlands, with perhaps a preference for those with wide rides and clearings; also, where unmolested, in wooded gardens or parks in towns.

APPEARANCE General impression from usual fleeting glimpse is of a mauvish-brown, jackdaw-sized bird with white rump and black tail. At rest most distinctive feature is bright blue, black-barred patch on fore-wing, against adjoining white area; wing-tips black. Head also a prominent feature, for greyish, dark-streaked crown feathers can be partially erected, and combined with black moustache and pale blue eye, total effect is somewhat baleful and intimidating. Young very similar, but duller and browner.

VOICE Usual call is loud, harsh 'kahk-kahk'; many other sounds, but commonest, used particularly in times of stress, a mewing indistinguishable from that of cat.

FOOD On the whole more vegetarian than magpie; almost any fruit or berries, wild or cultivated; peas and beans both when newly sown or sprouting, and in green stage when hacked from pods; acorns, nuts, beechmast (these also hoarded; probably jay, through habit of hiding tree-seeds in turf or moss, is chief natural agent for dispersal of these to distance from parent-trees). Animal matter very much as for magpie, including eggs and young—also a great destroyer of woodland-nesting pigeons, both eggs and young being taken.

NESTING Usual site not very high, in dense undergrowth rather than large trees. Nest of twigs, like rather small nest of wood pigeon from below, but of finer twigs, much more interwoven, and with well-formed cup neatly lined, almost invariably with root-fibres. 5–6 eggs, little larger than those of blackbird and very similar in colour—greenish with fine brownish markings, but almost always with at least one black line on big end.

4. Jay

The Starling

Although so common that its presence tends to be taken for granted, the starling can provide more all-the-year-round interest than any other comparably common species. In many ways it is a bird of contrasts: in plumage, which varies with age and with the season; in its relations with man, for it can be either a beneficial consumer of insect-pests, or, for a much briefer period, an orchard pest; it can be hated as a drab, marauding gangster at the bird-table, or, a few weeks later, admired as an iridescent herald of spring probing the turf among the first crocuses; it can be a source of wonder, as the unanimous manœuvres of smoke-like flocks are watched assembling to roost—and immediately the aerial display is over, the object of displeasure when public buildings are befouled or tree-plantations destroyed by the settled hordes.

The wheezy attempts at song from roof-ridge or chimney-pot at first seem too feeble for notice, yet they are beautified by the sheer ecstasy expressed in the attitude of the singer—head raised, yellow beak wide open, wings slightly ajar and drooping, and throat distended so that each quivering hackle is separated.

Although its special nesting requirements prevent it from being a large-scale colonial breeder, at all other seasons the starling is markedly gregarious. Flocking begins almost straight from the nest. The sudden appearance of assemblies of mouse-coloured juveniles and dark adults among the fading may-blossom is (for the early-riser) one of the landmarks of the year. Since the insistent 'cheer-cheer' food-call on such a day as this will no longer be heard from beneath urban eaves or rural thatch, but, now concentrated, is heard at the gathering-site, it can only be concluded that, in a given area, the vast majority of starling broods fly on the same day. It thus appears that the mysterious unanimity, which seems to control starlings in the mass, also exists when the birds are scattered in their nesting-sites, for the concerted arrival at maturity of the season's young must follow an equally well synchronised laying of the first eggs.

Soon after midsummer these post-breeding flocks begin to congregate at communal roosts. By late November some of these congregations, composed of feeding flocks from anything up to a twenty mile radius, may consist of millions of individuals, and without doubt, for sheer awe-inspiring number and uncanny mass-discipline, such phenomenal behaviour does not reach these magnificent proportions in any other British bird. Research has revealed that, although the winter population in rural areas is heavily augmented by immigrants from the continent, the well-known London roosts, such as that around Trafalgar Square, are composed of metropolitan and suburban residents.

Notes on The Starling

HAUNTS Equally at home in town or country. No doubt originally a forest-breeder, but alternative accommodation provided by buildings has enabled it to thrive away from ancestral woodland. Trees usually important source of caterpillar food for rearing young, but not essential—some populations breed on treeless islands. After breeding, a thorough forager of the ground—arable, grassland, playing-fields, marshes and edges of winter floods, sea-shores, refuse-dumps, sewage-disposal works.

APPEARANCE Body almost as large as that of blackbird, but much shorter tail and legs, and proportionately larger beak, result in impression of top-heavy dumpiness. Buff or white tips to feathers which cause speckled appearance in winter wear away to leave more uniform dark plumage in spring; thus glossy 'new' summer plumage is in fact threadbare winter outfit. Never completely black—some brown retained on flight feathers, and remainder black shot with purple, green, blue and red. Bill dark in winter, but changes to pale yellow in breeding plumage. No conspicuous differences between sexes in the field, but minor differences in shape of neck-feathers and bill-colour are revealed by birds in the hand. Young pass through confusing stage when moulting from juvenile to winter plumage—wearing varying mixtures of uniform buff with patches of darker new feathers. Gait very distinctive—a deliberate, rather pigeon-toed walk, sometimes speeded up into a run; can also hop rapidly.

VOICE A confused mixture of wheezes, gurgles and clicks, delivered from wide-open bill. Also prone to mimicry of phrases from songs and calls of other birds, and of less natural noises.

FOOD An omnivorous scavenger in populated areas, but basically a soil-prober in search of insect grubs; leatherjackets (larvae of cranefly) staple article of diet for most of year. Fond of fruit in season, particularly cherries and berries of elder and yew.

NESTING Only requisite a dark hole—hollow or woodpecker-hole in tree, cavities in buildings, or crannies in rock-face or quarries. Nest usually bulky mass of straw or hay, but with deep, feather lined cup. Normally 5 pale blue eggs.

5. Starling, winter (above),
summer (below)

The Greenfinch and
The Linnet

The Greenfinch   This is one of the commonest members of the mixed flocks of seed-eating birds—chaffinches, linnets, yellowhammers and tree sparrows—which roam stubbles and weedy wastes throughout autumn and winter, and in many areas it is the predominant species in such gatherings. Some of these vast flocks may be augmented by winter visitors, but judging by its present abundance as a breeding-species, local birds alone could account for the greenfinch numbers. Greenfinches in flocks such as these behave in a very predictable manner when suddenly disturbed: they rise in bouncing flight, uttering a rapid wheezy twitter, and tend to form into a pure flock of their own species; they then fly away, often to a considerable distance, and after much circling around, swooping low when passing and repassing the place from which they arose, they suddenly pitch down and silently resume their feeding—provided, of course, that the causer of the disturbance remains still.

The cock greenfinch is an extremely handsome bird, and its wheezy call, though monotonous, is as evocative of warm, idle hours as is the purring of the turtle dove; but its really outstanding claim to distinction is a performance which for some reason rarely seems to attract the attention which it deserves. This is the song-flight display, in which the greenfinch both looks and sounds, for a few brief moments, like a totally different species; the wings and tail are fully extended (thus displaying the yellow on each to the full) to form a continuous surface, and the bird performs a slow, wavering flight in a wide circle back to its perch again. During this 'bat-flight' a continuous stream of notes is emitted, starting with a rapid, wheezy twittering, but ending with several long notes, almost as pure and bell-like as those of a woodlark. Even in areas where greenfinches are very plentiful, such complete displays are not seen as frequently as would be expected; one is tempted to wonder whether this is in fact an essential part of mating in all cases, or merely the desperate last resort of some unattached cock. In any case it is a very efficacious form of advertisement, for subsequently a nest will be found in the circle encompassed by the display, usually near its centre.

The Linnet   This is our commonest member of the family of the small finches, which includes the goldfinch, the redpoll, the siskin and the twite. It may not be one of the gayest British birds in respect of fine feathers (although a cock in full plumage is decidedly smartly-clad), but it is certainly the gayest in demeanour. Its outstanding qualities (in human terms) seem to be light-heartedness with a very marked touch of eccentricity, combined with great energy and industry—or probably bustle would be a better word than the last. It prefers not to fly in a straight line from one point to another, even for a short distance, but indulges in what appear to be crazy flourishes of waverings and bouncings to embellish an otherwise uninteresting act; the same erratic flight behaviour, magnified a thousandfold, can be seen when a whole foraging flock is on the move—but here the sudden changes, of course, are remarkably concerted, as if a mass-eccentricity were now in control. Winter flocks of linnets, particularly in open country such as downland, heaths and commons, are usually of the one species alone, but on stubble, or on exceptional food-sources such as a few acres of mustard gone to seed and unharvested, they will join other finches.

Notes on The Greenfinch

HAUNTS In breeding-season open woodland or edges of denser woods, hedgerows, scrub, or gardens and parks where trees and shrubs present. Outside breeding-season wanders as already described.

APPEARANCE About sparrow-sized, but stockier and with stouter bill; plumage brownish-green, much yellower on rump, and bright yellow patches on wing and sides of tail; colours more highly developed in male, and in addition (in summer plumage) grey on wing and dark tips to wing and tail-feathers are prominent; young have yellow on wing and tail, but dark-streaked breasts; all have distinctly notched tail.

VOICE Normal call a drawn-out 'sweer' or 'sweeze' almost two-syllabled. For song, delivered from perch or (more elaborated) in song-flight, see main text.

FOOD Weed-seed of many kinds—as fond of fluffy composite seeds as goldfinch; corn gleaned from stubble or stack-yard; and very fond of pips extracted from remains of fallen apples after black-birds and starlings have removed pulp.

NESTING Nests in hedgerow or garden bushes, or small trees (including conifers) in open plantations; nest of moss, fine twigs and fibres, often bulky, but with neat cup lined with hair and sometimes few feathers or fragments of wool. 5–6 eggs, whitish or pale bluish-green, lightly marked with reddish spots and streaks.

Notes on The Linnet

HAUNTS Furzy commons, open scrub of thorn or juniper, most typical breeding-haunts, where almost colonial; also hedges and garden bushes. Flocks roam open country after breeding, but many emigrate, particularly to Landes area of south-west France.

APPEARANCE Male in breeding plumage distinguished by crimson on breast and crown, grey head, chestnut brown of upper wing and back, and greyish-white feathers on edge of wing and tail; female lacks crimson, and is generally duller, but with similar wing and tail pattern; young like female, but streakier plumage; all have marked cleft in tail.

VOICE Flight-call a rapid, almost harsh 'zee-chee-chee'; song, on wing or from perch, an elaboration of this call mingled with fluting and vibrant notes, often long-sustained and pleasantly musical.

FOOD Mainly weed-seeds, but also small-seeded field-crops such as linseed and mustard. Nestlings fed on insect larvae.

NESTING Usually low in dense bush; nest of grass-stems and similar fine fibres, lined with hair and wool. Usually 5 eggs, like those of greenfinch but smaller.

6. Linnet, male (above). Greenfinch, males (below)

The Goldfinch

If one had to choose a bird to substitute for a berry in Dr Butler's famous dictum about the strawberry, this one would come high on the list, for few would contradict a sentiment such as 'Doubtless God could have made a more pleasing bird, but doubtless God never did'. In every respect it seems to meet with human approval. It has colourful plumage—gold, crimson, black and white and buff; a cheerfully pleasant song; a light-hearted demeanour with an endearing touch of eccentricity; is not shy of man, and indeed often seems to prefer his artificial surroundings, whether tidy flower-borders or neglected weed-patches; it is markedly sociable; is a superb craftsman in nest-building; and, almost too good to be true, has no habits which arouse the enmity of farmer, gardener or gamekeeper. At one time these very virtues almost brought about its downfall, for thanks to its popularity as a cage-bird, and the ease with which it could be lured into captivity, its numbers were seriously reduced by the bird-catcher before it was given legal protection.

Like the red grouse and the heather family, or the crossbill and conifers, the goldfinch has a peculiar association with one group of plants, the Natural Order *Compositæ*. But this has not the same restrictive effect upon the distribution of the goldfinch, for almost one-third of all the species of flowering plants in the world happen to belong to the family of its choice, and there are few habitats, wild or garden, where some plants with daisy-type flowers do not grow in abundance. But the association of gold-finches with composite flowers goes further than the provision of the seed which is their staple article of diet, for the fluff from the seeds of certain species is an almost essential nesting material.

After leaving the nest, 'charms' of goldfinches, beginning with family parties of six or seven, but uniting with others until much larger assemblies are formed, roam the countryside. Since the breeding season is protracted, two broods being usual and three not uncommon, by early autumn a charm in favourable feeding areas may consist of over two hundred birds. Such concentrations occur where overgrazing or drought have allowed pastures to be overrun by seeding thistles, or in that goldfinch paradise—temporary wasteland where thistles, teasels, sow-thistles and wild lettuce run riot.

These flocks usually disappear by late autumn, and by midwinter, although single birds, or twos and threes may be seen, large gatherings are exceptional. There is growing evidence from the recovery of British-ringed goldfinches from south-west France and Spain that many, perhaps the majority, of our native birds emigrate southwards at the approach of winter.

Notes on The Goldfinch

HAUNTS Hedges, gardens, parks, waste-land, orchards.

APPEARANCE In flight gold-barred wing, transparent white patches on wing and tail, bouncing flight almost always accompanied by sweet twitter, sociability and general erratic, restless behaviour all make this an easy species for identification. At rest (and feeding birds will often allow approach to within a few yards) unmistakable features are: crimson around base of bill, reaching to eye; black and white wing barred bright yellow; blackish tail with distinctive white spots at tip.

VOICE A very rapid 'swit-sweet' twitter, liquid rather than wheezy; not loud, yet with remarkable carrying-power. Almost invariably an accompaniment to flight and, on a much more excited scale, often the first indication of presence of feeding party. Song an improved version of this twitter, with notes of a more tinkling, canary-like quality.

FOOD Mainly seeds of composite flowers in season—coltsfoot, groundsel, dandelion, sow-thistle and most species of thistle; favourite garden plants are cornflower, sweet sultan, cosmea, single China asters and Michaelmas daisy. Garden lettuce allowed to seed are a sure attraction. Fluffy pappus bitten off seeds when feeding. Only non-composite which is commonly frequented is teasel. Over-wintering birds, when ground supply of teasel, burdock and thistle is scarce or snow-covered, will resort to tree-seed, particularly that of alder and birch.

NESTING Usually in small fork at extreme tip of branch, often near crown of tree. Fruit trees, especially apple, together with horse chestnut, greatly favoured, but will frequently nest in hawthorn and sycamore. Nest extremely neat and compact; a small, tightly woven cup of fibres, moss, cobweb and wool, often with outside finish of lichen, with lining of felted plant-down. First clutch of 5–6 bluish-white eggs, sparsely marked with reddish-brown, usually laid in May, but nesting season may extend to late August. Young fed on regurgitated seed-mash; but small caterpillars and other insects seen to be taken by parents at this period; feeding visits to nest not frequent—presumably mode of feeding ensures large helpings.

7. Goldfinch

The Bullfinch

Although fruit-growers who have suffered from the depredations of the bullfinch might agree that its name could be a corruption of budfinch, its present name, however derived, seems sufficiently apt, for there is something bull-like about the thick-set build and somewhat pugnacious aspect of this bird. In character, however, it fails to live up to its name, for it is one of the shyest and most secretive of birds—so much so that, once the observer has been alerted by the fluting call, the commonest view obtained is of a bird with a conspicuous white rump retreating into the nearest cover. But, wherever there are plums, pears, peaches, almonds, Japanese quince, forsythia or gooseberries visible from indoors, sooner or later, in town or country, the householder is almost certain to have an opportunity to watch this handsome bird at close quarters.

Admiration mingled with exasperation is the usual reaction, but there are some extremists who willingly accept the fleeting beauty of such visitations, even at the cost of blossom-less shrubs and fruit-less trees. But commercial fruit-growers cannot afford such high æsthetic standards, and no one who has seen the complete barrenness of a plum-orchard following a few days' attention from bullfinches in the preceding winter, can fail to understand why, in such areas, this bird is no longer on the protected list. But tremendous slaughter in fruit-growing areas seems to have done little to reduce numbers, and since the years in which bullfinches become pests are rarely consecutive, it seems unlikely that this method of control will succeed.

It might be thought that years of widespread bullfinch damage must correspond with peaks in bullfinch population, and that years of respite are indications of poor breeding seasons and lowered numbers; but this does not seem to be the case. The plump flower-buds of trees and shrubs are apparently a secondary or reserve diet only resorted to when the staple winter food, the seeds of a few favoured species of trees, are not available. Thus in the snow-bound winter of 1962–63, in an area where bullfinches had done much damage in the previous winter, the feared invasion of the orchard never came, and at first it was assumed that there was none in the vicinity. Tell-tale evidence of empty ash-keys beneath a tree not two hundred yards away led to the discovery of a daily feeding flock of about twenty birds. Just as this food was nearly finished, the thaw came and exposed an untouched ground supply of the next most popular seeds, those of sycamore and maple. A bumper crop of plums, pears and peaches followed.

When watching a bullfinch dealing with such large-kernelled tree-seeds the function of the specialised thick bill and wide gape becomes apparent. The fruit is manipulated by bill and tongue until the flat seed-bearing portion is vertical; pressure is then applied, and the surrounding envelope splits; a flick of the thick tongue, and the seed is extracted and the empty case ejected.

Notes on The Bullfinch

HAUNTS   In breeding season woods, large hedges or shrubberies, provided that some dense cover, e.g. evergreens or blackthorn thicket, is available. In winter and spring gardens and orchards, but also weedy wastes where it may accompany other finches.

APPEARANCE   About sparrow-sized, but with stouter body and shorter legs. Both sexes recognisable by black cap, black, grey-barred wing, very conspicuous white rump-patch, and black tail. Wide, deep but short bill, and rather flat crown form profile that is unmistakable. The male has well demarcated colour zones—uniform pale grey back, brick-pink underparts meeting black crown on level with eye; whiteness of rump accentuated by glossy black of tail and wing. General pattern of female as for male, but duller and less clear-cut colours. Young lack black caps, and are altogether browner, but already have distinctive rump, wing and tail markings.

VOICE   A musical, rather plaintive fluting call 'pew-pew' or 'pew-pew-pew'; soft, yet carries well. No true song, although slight variations of call notes may be detected in breeding season.

FOOD   Mainly vegetable; in addition to seeds and buds already referred to, also fond of composite seeds—groundsel, dandelion and sow thistle. Too heavy to perch on these as goldfinch does, and therefore often overlooked when feeding on groundsel among weed-cover. Young fed by regurgitation—insects, spiders and even small snails usually present in general mash of seed and salad. In winter some berries eaten, those of privet especially.

NESTING   Dense thickets or bushes of many species; favourites are blackthorn, box, philadelphus, snow-berry. Nest often comparatively flimsy structure of fine twigs, but always with well-made deep cup of fine root-fibres with sometimes a little hair. Eggs greenish-blue, with spots and streaks of purplish-brown, mainly at big end. Two broods are normally raised each season.

8. Bullfinch, male (above), female (below)

The Chaffinch

At the last attempt to make a population census of British breeding birds, some thirty years ago, this species and the blackbird tied for top place as our most abundant land-birds. The situation is very different to-day, for although it is probable that the blackbird would still occupy its leading position, there is no doubt that the chaffinch would be much lower in the list. The decline, which took place before the bird-killing winter of 1962–63, has been most marked in agricultural areas, and since it coincided with the widespread use of highly toxic chemicals as seed-dressings, it seems reasonable to suspect that this is the explanation. The suspicion is strengthened by the fact that, together with the wood pigeon and the house sparrow, the chaffinch was one of the commonest species found dead or dying during these holocausts of the early 1960s. The chaffinch is (or was) a common nester in gardens, and during the rearing of its young is a useful controller of pests, particularly aphids and fruit-tree caterpillars. Unfortunately, at this critical period it, and its offspring, may again be exposed to the risk of poisoning, for (although the wielder of the sprayer is usually unaware of the fact) the same types of persistent poisons which rendered the seed-dressings so deadly are the active ingredients of most modern garden insecticides. There are signs that the decline is now rising from its trough, but the rate of recovery is much slower than that of the robuster greenfinch.

Certainly the chaffinch is one of the most desirable of garden birds. The cock bird's plumage—grey-blue cap, steely bill, pink-brown breast, flashing white shoulders and tail feathers—is striking and conspicuous, but elegant rather than gaudy. Its cheerful and much-repeated song, from mid-February onwards, is one of the first real signs of the approach of spring. Its nest is one of the most meticulously constructed to be found in Britain, ranking in miniature perfection with that of the long-tailed tit and goldcrest. In town or city park the chaffinch is equally appreciated, for in addition to the attractive qualities already listed, it is as fearless and cheeky a scavenger for crumbs around the park-benches as the ubiquitous sparrow.

The hey-day of the country chaffinch was undoubtedly before the advent of the combine-harvester. Its name suggests that it was a forager for weed seeds among the chaff winnowed from the threshing-floor in the days of the flail, but the era of the stack-yard and the threshing-machine attracted the truly great congregations. Such winter flocks may still be seen on weedy stubble or, most attractive focus of all, a field of unharvested mustard, but these are often augmented by winter visitors. A striking feature of such gatherings is that they may be of one sex only—hence its Linnaean name *Fringilla coelebs*, the bachelor finch.

In spite of one vernacular name, pea-finch, the chaffinch is not a garden pest; another name, wheat-finch, might be taken to mean what it says from the evidence of the seed-dressing slaughter. Both, in fact, refer to the conspicuous flash of white in the plumage, and are derived from pied finch and white finch respectively.

Notes on The Chaffinch

HAUNTS A bird of open woodland (including mature pine-forest) and edges of woodland, which has readily accepted man-made substitutes for its original habitat—hedges, gardens, parks, street avenues, and early stages of coniferous plantations.

APPEARANCE The male has blue-grey head, pinkish-brown breast, white very noticeable on broad shoulder-flash, narrower wing-bar and outer tail-feathers; colours, particularly blue of head, duller in winter. The female lacks bright colours of male, but recognisable by same pattern of white in wing and tail.

VOICE Call a metallic 'pink, pink'. Song usually delivered from fairly high perch on tree (sometimes from buildings)—begins with deliberate 'chip-chip-chip' rapidly accelerating, and ending with loud, hurried flourish.

FOOD Mainly seeds, both from weeds and trees such as alder, pine, larch and spruce. Will occasionally take small berries such as red-currants. Small insects such as aphids, and small moth-caterpillars (especially from fruit-trees and oaks), main food of young in nest, but also figure largely in adults' diet in spring and early summer.

NESTING Nest often well-concealed in fork of tree-branch, but just as often in twigs of hawthorn hedge or small bush; will nest in conifers, from tall spruce to dwarf juniper. Nest a compact cup, usually of moss with some cobweb and lichen on outside; outside finish resembles that of long-tailed tit's nest, but more daring in adding oddments of decorative bric-à-brac such as coloured wool or scraps of paper. Well-lined, usually with hair. Clutch normally of 5 eggs, brownish-green or bluish-green, with dark brown blotches and scribbles.

9. Chaffinch, male (above), female (below)

The House Sparrow and the Tree Sparrow

The House Sparrow   A test of public opinion would almost certainly nominate this bird as the species most plentiful in Britain; but it would be wrong, for in total population it is far outnumbered by many other species. The impression that it is ubiquitous is a reflection on its chief characteristic—its dependence on man for both food and shelter, which has resulted in its becoming a successful hanger-on of man in village, town and city. In uncultivated and sparsely inhabited areas it is therefore scarce, and often completely absent. One would have expected that the town or city sparrow would have declined as literal horse-power was replaced by its mechanical equivalent, for the stables, spilt corn and chaff from nose-bags, and the droppings themselves, were sure sources of food in the days of horse-drawn traffic. But the amount of waste food to be scavenged wherever humans congregate, and the help given by householders who throw out scraps, to say nothing of the more deliberate feeding from the park-bench, have all enabled the sparrow to survive and thrive as a city-dweller.

Taking the bestowal of a 'Christian' name as a criterion, the house sparrow, in spite of its depredations among the ripening grain, must at one time have been regarded with some affection, for in medieval and Tudor times it was always 'Phillip' or 'Phip' Sparrow. Even when corn-growers in the homeland were paying out 'sparrow money' for birds killed and eggs taken, emigrants were taking caged specimens to the Americas and the Antipodes. From these victims of 'transportation' and from some more deliberate introductions, the house sparrow is now established in every continent but one; but it is significant of this bird's ability to thrive wherever man can exist that the greatest authority on this species cautiously states that 'it has not *yet* colonised Antarctica'. From its uninhibited display of ardour in courtship and mating, and the noisy pursuits of gangs of cocks after a single hen bird, the sparrow, while admired for its perkiness and tenacity, has also been frowned upon as a low and disreputable character.

The Tree Sparrow   The names alone do not sufficiently differentiate between our two sparrows, for the house sparrow will often roost and nest in trees and bushes, and the tree sparrow will sometimes nest in buildings. But on the whole the tree sparrow is much less dependent on man and his activities, and is a correspondingly scarcer, and certainly a much less well-known, species. It is most noticeable in winter, when it roams about either in pure flocks of from tens to hundreds, or more frequently in association with finches and other seed-eating species. It has a marked affinity with yellow-hammers in winter, not only feeding with them on stubbles and weedy wastes, but also in sharing the same roosts in tall hedges. Unlike the house sparrow it is not a bird-table frequenter, although in areas where it is plentiful it is a common user of nest-boxes. It is altogether a neater bird than its commoner relative, slightly smaller and decidedly slimmer, and is more obviously a wild, as opposed to a semi-domesticated bird. Another point of difference, which simplifies identification, is that there are no variations in

49

plumage, depending on age and sex, such as are observable in a party of house sparrows, for the completely brown caps and double wing-bars are worn by all tree-sparrows, whether adult cocks and hens or juvenile birds of the year.

Its abundance in winter in some inland areas, where it is not regarded as a common breeding species, does not seem to be due to influxes from any great distance, but merely to the fact that it is so easily overlooked when dispersed in the same neighbourhood during the nesting season. Like the house sparrow, it tends to be a colonial breeder, but since its nesting requirements—hollow trees—do not normally occur in such close proximity as houses, its scope in this respect is limited; rows or clumps of old pollard willows, however, or even a liberal supply of nest-boxes, will attract considerable concentrations of breeding pairs.

Notes on The House Sparrow

HAUNTS Never far from human habitations.

APPEARANCE Distinguished from other brownish seed-eating birds by lack of white on tail-feathers. Male has grey crown bordered by brown, off-white cheeks and black throat; rump grey as crown, and short but noticeable white wing-bar. Female and young lack grey and black of male.

VOICE Call a loud 'cheep' or 'chippip', or a rapid, harsh twitter. Chirping may be developed into a series with squeaky or almost purring trills, which may be called an elementary form of song.

FOOD A seed (and predominantly grain) eater which has readily adapted itself, when necessary, to other mainly farinaceous substitutes. But in breeding-season, particularly where woodland, gardens and orchards available, insects, particular caterpillars and aphids, form important contribution to diet.

NESTING Perfect nest, such as not infrequently built in branches of trees, a completely domed, untidy structure of hay and straw, with side entrance; well-lined with feathers. Nests in buildings, now commonest site, simulate this according to space available, some domed, some partially so, and others merely lined cavities. 4–6 eggs, very variable, most commonly pale greyish with fine dark spotting all over.

Notes on The Tree Sparrow

HAUNTS Farmland rather than uncultivated areas, or willowed river-valleys, and gardens (even suburban) within reach of arable land for winter foraging.

APPEARANCE See main text.

VOICE Very like that of house sparrow, except that flight-note from flocks is a harsh 'keck-keck' call. Song is short, deliberate twitter with occasional chirrup. Not so persistently vocal as house sparrow.

FOOD Very much as for house sparrow—perhaps larger proportion of weed-seeds.

NESTING Mainly in holes or hollows in trees, sometimes in thatch, ricks or sheds. Nest, like house sparrows, but never domed, and since often in cramped cavity less material used. 4–6 eggs, noticeably smaller and browner than those of house sparrow.

10. Tree Sparrow (above). House Sparrow, male (middle), female (below)

The Skylark

For a songbird (using the term to embrace all perching-birds, irrespective of the quality of some of the sounds which serve as song) some eminence from which to sing, whether the orchard bough for the chaffinch or a mere clod of earth for the corn-bunting, seems an essential need. Some species, such as the whitethroat and the greenfinch, and to a much higher degree the pipits, do indulge in song in mid-air, but the spells are of brief duration, and the flight-display is as important as the song. But only the skylark (among British birds) has developed this delivery of song from on the wing to such a pitch that some almost static point high in the sky is its substitute for a singing-perch. As with the meadow pipit, this is obviously an adaptation to life in surroundings where trees and bushes may be entirely lacking, or if present are so sparse that they are insufficient in proportion to the otherwise suitable land available for breeding. Much of a skylark's daily life is therefore spent in the air, and the large broad wing is accordingly quite disproportionate to the size of its body, for although its body is little bulkier than that of a sparrow, its wing-span is about equal to that of a starling. The corresponding and contrasting adaptation to fit it for life in its preferred haunts is that for all other activities—feeding, nesting and roosting—it has become essentially a ground-bird. Although it can perch, and may occasionally begin its song from a fence before launching itself upward, its long, straight hind-claw (the 'larkspur' of the flower name) is typical of the bird-foot used for walking and standing, rather than hopping and perching.

As with other outstanding songsters, the skylark is intensely territorial, and the frequent chases and skirmishes, often just above ground level, which occur in the breeding season, although the source of the term 'skylarking' for light-hearted and aimless human activities, are in fact serious demonstrations to establish or maintain territorial rights.

Like the lapwing, the skylark is to be seen all the year round in suitable country, but, as is also the case with the lapwing, the chances are that the birds observed may not be the same individuals, for the bulk of our breeding-population moves southward in autumn, and its place is taken by immigrants from the north and east. Parties of the latter (or native birds on passage to further south), passing over in widely spaced formation, are regularly to be seen throughout September and October. Even when the birds are too high to be seen clearly by the unaided eye, the frequent flight-call—a 'chirrup' with a distinctive watery quality—and the peculiar mode of flight, which always looks as if it were a struggle against a head-wind, together leave no doubt as to the species on the move.

Notes on The Skylark

HAUNTS   Open country, dry, damp or wet — arable land, meadow or downland grass, grassy marshland, sand-dunes, moors, mountains and bogs; requirements very similar to those of lapwing, but skylark will tolerate longer grass and ground-vegetation.

APPEARANCE   On ground walking gait, combined with brown back streaked buff, and pale underparts dark-streaked on throat and breast, and especially slight but noticeable crest, distinguish from other small ground-feeders; although surprisingly small after having been seen in flight, much larger and stockier than similarly-coloured meadow pipit. In flight broad wing and white outer tail-feathers, noticeable; on typical song-flight identifiable by this alone.

VOICE   Mode of delivery and long-sustained nature of song (often minutes, rather than seconds of other species) have probably given the song a poetic appeal which would not occur if similar sounds were emitted in short snatches from bird hidden in foliage; but undeniably a very pleasing mixture of shrill warblings, accentuated by wing-action which seems to be pumping the melody out.

FOOD   About equally animal and vegetable matter; grubs, worms, snails, spiders, seeds of corn and weeds; also 'salad', particularly first leaves of seedlings.

NESTING   Though on ground, a true nest built, usually of grass lined with finer fibres; normally well-concealed in hollow or beneath grass-tuft. 4–5 eggs, dirty-white or greyish, heavily and evenly speckled with darker markings.

The Pied Wagtail and the Grey Wagtail

The Pied Wagtail This bird, conspicuous, elegant and partial to human environments, is probably better known than many much more plentiful species. An additional factor which makes it hard to overlook is that although a passerine (a perching-bird), it spends most of its waking hours on the ground—particularly lawns, yards or margins of waters—or often on roofs and buildings, so that it is normally in the open, well away from concealing foliage. It has become so adapted to a life on the ground that its normal method of progress, instead of the hop of a typical passerine, is a rapid walk or run—hence John Clare's 'little trotty wagtail'. The mannerism from which it gets its name (although the long tail is bobbed up and down, rather than wagged from side to side) is not reserved for any special function such as display, but is an intermittent accompaniment to most routine activities except flight; the purpose served by this seemingly nervous habit still awaits a satisfactory explanation.

Although during the breeding season pairs are normally so well spaced out that they seldom give the impression of a large total population, in late summer and early autumn they may suddenly become abundant in some areas. This is usually an indication that somewhere in the neighbourhood a communal roost, most often in a reed-bed, has been formed. These are usually at their peak when swallows, preparing for emigration, are making temporary use of similar roosts, and indeed the two species frequently occupy the same reed-bed; but although a fair proportion of the wagtails may leave to winter in south-west Europe, many remain to occupy the roosts throughout the winter.

A very typical piece of feeding-behaviour, to be seen when this wagtail is searching for insects on lawns, is a vertical leap, usually of only a few inches, into the air to snap a flying insect; this is sometimes extended into a long aerial pursuit on a more even keel, presumably when the 'vertical take-off' technique has failed and the size of the quarry makes the expenditure of further energy worthwhile.

The Grey Wagtail Although the pied wagtail is often called the 'water' wagtail, it is the grey wagtail which is the more entitled to the name; perhaps 'waterfall' wagtail would be even more appropriate, for the water with which it is almost invariably associated is usually water in rapid motion. 'Grey', with its suggestion of neutral drabness, is also not a very descriptive name, for its pastel-shades of grey and yellow (enhanced by black in the male), together with its graceful proportions, make this one of the most beautiful of British birds. To be seen at its best it should be poised, long tail bobbing, on some small projection close to the surface of slack water, for then the underparts are mirrored, revealing the richest yellow of all—bright chrome with almost a hint of orange—at the base of the body beneath the tail.

Its general habits are very much like those of the pied wagtail, except that it makes greater use of the surface of water as a source of food—for this purpose it will drop from a perch into a momentary hover just above the water; it also more habitually catches insects in the air. When both grey wagtails and mayfly were common the hatch of the latter provided ideal opportunities for observing both methods of feeding—a constant shuttling upwards and downwards, as dancing or spent prey alternately attracted the attention of the feeder.

At one time, in southern England, this wagtail was mainly a winter visitor from the mountain and moorland streams of the north and north-west where it had bred; but from about 1930 onwards it extended its breeding-range southwards so progressively that within twenty years it had become an expected spring and summer adornment of locks and weirs throughout the Home Counties. A catastrophic halt to this welcome spread of breeding-population was called by the winter of 1962–63, for the grey wagtail, judging by its ensuing absence from old haunts and the scarcity of wintering birds, must have been one of the most hard-hit of all species.

Notes on The Pied Wagtail

HAUNTS — Open country, with marked preference for habitats shaped by man—lawns, playing-fields, parks, farms, sewage-works—all made more attractive if water in the vicinity; such surroundings also supply variety of artificial nesting-sites.

APPEARANCE — Black, white and grey plumage, long bobbing tail, ground-haunting habits and bouncing flight, all make identification easy. Juveniles can be confusing, as not yet pied, but mainly buff and grey; parts which will eventually be white, particularly on face, yellowish; but dark crescentic breast-band, general shape and behaviour clinch identification.

VOICE — Call, much used in flight as well as at rest, a clear, sharp 'chizzick'. Song, usually accompanied by short display-flight, a mixture of call notes and rapid chirrupping—but very feeble and audible only at close range.

FOOD — Mainly insects, or minute crustaceans from water's edge, but seeds eaten in winter.

NESTING — Cavities of all kinds—in banks, walls, pollard willows, timber-stacks, ricks, creepers on walls, empty receptacles lying on ground. Nest of moss, dead leaves or similar artificial materials, lined with hair and feathers. About 5 eggs, greyish with darker freckling all over.

Notes on The Grey Wagtail

HAUNTS — For breeding haunts see main text; in winter often around sewage-works and reservoirs.

APPEARANCE — Although about same length as pied wagtail, appears slimmer and longer, owing to greater length of tail. Back pale blue-grey, upper breast pale yellow, becoming deeper beneath tail; in breeding-plumage male has black throat and bib; both sexes have whitish eye-stripe and white outer tail-feathers.

VOICE — Both call and song closely resemble that of pied wagtail.

FOOD — Similar to that of pied wagtail, except that higher proportion of aquatic insects, in all stages, eaten.

NESTING — Usually in bank or rock-crevice near water, or similar artificial sites in structure of locks, weirs and mills. Nest of moss and fibres, hair-lined; about 5 eggs, browner than those of pied.

12. Pied Wagtail (above). Grey Wagtail, female (middle), male (below)

The Tree Creeper and the Nuthatch

These two are oddities among British birds, for although their typical mode of progress—up, around or along the trunks and branches of trees—suggests some relationship to the woodpeckers, they are in fact highly adapted members of the passerine order, the large group containing all our perching-birds from raven to wren.

The Tree Creeper   But for the brief flit from tree to tree, this mouse-like bird is seldom seen doing anything other than living up to its name. Its feeding procedure is very stereotyped; it alights at the base of a trunk, ascends it in jerky spirals, stops every so often to probe in crannies, branches off to do the same on secondary limbs, and finally flies down to start all over again from the base of another tree. Even when accompanying roving parties of tits in winter, it still tends to pay more attention to bark than to twigs and buds.

Although a common visitor to gardens with mature trees, and sociable with tits, its specialised requirements are not catered for by the normal bird-table; but unnatural food such as dripping or cheese is eagerly taken—provided that it is smeared on bark. When climbing the tree creeper presses its stiff tail against the bark, woodpecker fashion. It is rarely seen on the ground. Even at roost it does not behave like a perching bird, but presses itself, upright and face inwards, into some suitable cavity in rough bark or rotten wood. The furry, fibrous bark of the North American Big Tree or Wellingtonia, because it is soft enough to be excavated even by the tree creeper's slender bill, is especially favoured, and is almost certain to be used as a roost, often communally, by any tree creepers in its neighbourhood.

The Nuthatch   As it is a regular visitor to bird-tables in suitable areas, and will also build in nest-boxes, this is better-known than the tree creeper, particularly in the southern half of England. It easily becomes fearless, even to the extent of taking nuts from the hand. Its stocky, short-tailed build and powerful pointed beak give it a woodpecker-like appearance, but, unlike the tree creeper, it has not developed a stiff woodpecker tail. The uniform blue-grey of the back is such a striking feature that novice bird-watchers, encountering it for the first time, have been known to report a kingfisher at the bird-table.

In its natural habitat—deciduous woodland with mature timber—the nuthatch is usually first detected by its voice, for it is rarely silent at any time of the year. Its calls are varied, sometimes loud and wild, sometimes soft and soothing, but always clear, musical and of great carrying-power. The wild, cheerful spring song, the 'pay-pay-pay' whistle which is so deliberate that one imagines that the singer is counting the notes, is usually delivered from a formal display-posture with head raised and beak pointing skywards, and throat and chest puffed out.

The nuthatch shares with the song thrush the distinction of being a regular tool-user. Just as the thrush will bring snails from some distance to a favourite anvil-stone, so will the nuthatch bring its food for preparation to some rough-barked tree whose crannies will serve as vices. Such a vice-tree, usually oak or elm, is not difficult to find, for the familiar sound of a nuthatch hammering at a nut to 'hatch' it open will often lead one to this. The emptied remains still left wedged in the vice also afford evidence as to the nature of this bird's food; in addition to the expected nuts and acorns, one will often find oak marble-galls from which the grubs have been extracted.

Notes on The Tree Creeper

HAUNTS   Woodland, parks, gardens, old orchards, riverside willows—in short, anywhere with mature or old trees.

APPEARANCE   Not much larger than wren, but loose plumage and long tail make it appear much bigger. Upper plumage streaked with various shades of brown, rump uniform ginger-brown; distinctive pale buff wing-bar, whitish eye-stripe. Underparts silvery off-white. Beak long, thin and down-curved. Stiff, quilly tail. Rarely seen in sustained flight, but even on short, bouncing tree-to-tree flits, pale, almost transparent, wing-bar very noticeable.

VOICE   A shrill 'tzee-tzee' call, also a softer but penetrating rapid 'zit-zit-zit'; latter reminiscent of hard cloth being cut by fast-working tailor's scissors. Song, uttered while climbing or on wing, a mixture of the call notes, elaborated to finish with hurried trill or flourish.

FOOD   Small insects, together with their eggs, larvae and pupae; also spiders and woodlice.

NESTING   Usually a tight fit between loose bark and trunk; sometimes in similar situations in buildings, as behind loose boarding of shed. Nest well-built of fine twigs, moss and fibres, deep cup lined with feathers, wool, fragments of rotten wood and bark. 5–7 eggs, white with heavy reddish-brown spotting at large end.

Notes on The Nuthatch

HAUNTS   Woodland and well-timbered parks and gardens. But thins out northwards and uncommon north of line from Mersey to Humber.

APPEARANCE   Only climber with blue-grey back. Underparts—whitish on throat and cheeks, breast pinkish-buff colour intensifying downwards until almost orange-rust on flanks and belly. Bold, almost fierce effect produced by black stripe through eye. Unlike woodpeckers, can walk down tree headfirst.

VOICE   Commonest call a loud, deliberate, and somewhat explosive 'twit-twit-twit'. Song (apart from that mentioned earlier) a thrush-like 'twee-twee-twee', usually with distinct pauses between each group of three or four notes. Also a rapid song which can only be described as a mixture of churring and trilling.

FOOD   Nuts, acorns, beechmast, yew-seeds; also some insects from galls.

NESTING   A hole-nester, old borings of woodpeckers particularly favoured. Unique habit of plastering up hole with mud and wood-chips until aperture of required diameter remains. Nest little more than some dead leaves and lining of soft wood chippings and bark fibres; 5–8 eggs, white heavily marked with reddish-brown.

13.   Nuthatch, female (above),
male (middle).
Tree Creeper (below)

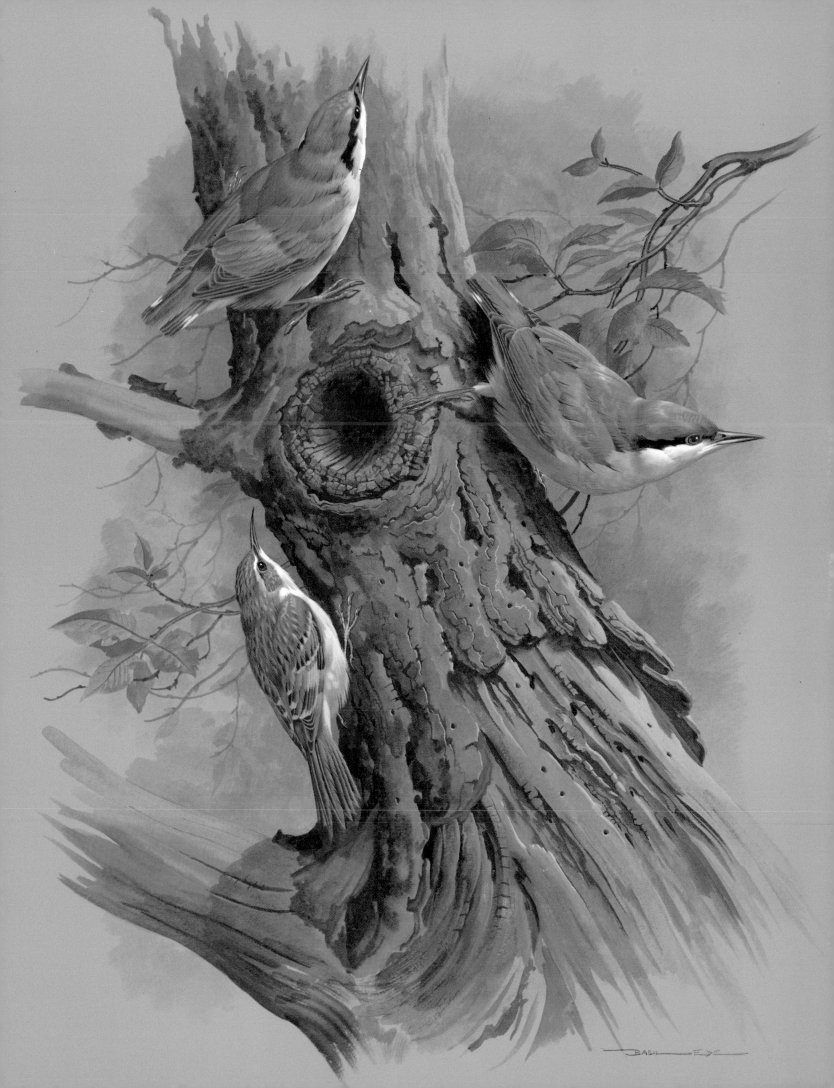

The Blue Tit and the
Great Tit

Of the four common tits in Britain these two are probably the most numerous, and certainly the best known, since they have readily taken advantage of the tits' welfare state created by the human provision of both food and housing. Apart from their bright colours, it is probably their industrious and acrobatic methods of feeding which add to their charm at the bird-table. They also display some power akin to intelligence when coping with problems, exhibited both in their exploitation of feeding-devices and in the opening of milk-bottles. Experimental work with tits has shown that, once they have discovered, by a process of trial and error, how to obtain food accessible only after a series of mechanical operations, they can remember the sequence of the steps in the rewarding procedure, which may involve the pulling of strings and the opening of miniature drawers.

The motive behind the uncapping of milk-bottles is obvious, but occasionally there are what seem to be infectious epidemics of destructive activity, such as the stripping of wallpaper or the tearing of books and letters, which seem to have no purpose. The tearing of papery bark is indulged in by tits both in search of food and in the gathering of materials for nest-building. Since paper-tearing seems to be commonest in residential areas, it has been suggested that this activity is directly connected with the bird-table. The theory is that wild tits are used to expending a certain amount of energy per day in seeking food; if the latter is obtainable without work, as at the feeding-table, the surplus energy still has to be expended, and paper-tearing, very similar to a food-seeking technique, is one outlet.

Outside the breeding season the activities of hurriedly roving flocks, mainly of these two species, would suggest a very fluid and nomadic population. The marking of birds which come to a feeding-table might also suggest the same situation, for hundreds of individuals may be found to have visited it in the course of a year, although the daily average may be only around half a dozen. The reappearance of known individuals, often three, sometimes five, and at least on one occasion ten years after their first appearance, with no recorded visits during the intervening years, would also suggest wanderings far afield. Yet all the evidence leads to a contrary conclusion, and these two species are in fact practically static, rarely moving more than a few miles from their native haunts. Exceptions occur, as in the autumn and winter of 1957, when several ringed individuals, known to be British natives, were found to have moved from 30–135 miles, all approximately in a northern direction. The explanation is that this coincided with a phenomenal irruption of tits from the Continent, and the assumption is that local birds were swept up by the invading hordes as they proceeded northwards.

Both these birds are useful inhabitants of the garden nest-box, for when rearing their numerous young they can be observed bringing in beakfuls of caterpillars, particularly from fruit-trees; they are both consumers of aphids, and the blue tit particularly will often hover to gather mealy aphis from beneath plum-leaves. The blue tit also has an eye for good quality fruit, and the choicest pears, apples and peaches are often spoilt by its small punctures. The great tit, having a comparatively powerful bill which can deal with nuts, finds no difficulty in opening a pea-pod to get at its contents, but this, fortunately, is an occasional rather than a regular feeding-habit. The great tit can have predatory feeding habits, which come very near to cannibalism; one was once watched entering a garden nest-box intended for its kind, but which a house sparrow had occupied, and which earlier that morning had been known to contain five newly-hatched young. The great tit emerged with a naked pink morsel in its beak, and the nest-box was found to have only two left. A return visit with a similar outcome was observed soon afterwards and at the next examination the sparrow's nest was empty.

Notes on The Blue Tit

HAUNTS Woodland, gardens, parks, hedges, orchards, riverside willows; in winter also frequently in reed-beds or similar masses of gone-to-seed vegetation.

APPEARANCE Unmistakable—no other small British bird has almost cobalt-blue plumage on head, wings and tail; white border to crown and white cheeks accentuate blueness of cap.

VOICE Call a thin 'tsee-tsee', but many variations. Song, rapid version of this, but with distinct trill towards end 'tsee-tsee-tsee-tsirrup-tsee'. Explosive spitting hiss from sitting bird if disturbed.

FOOD Catholic tastes at bird-table—seeds, nuts, fat, meat, cheese and bread—all indications of natural omnivorous habits. Largely insects (caterpillars, aphids, weevils) during breeding season, and insect eggs and pupae from trees in winter; also spiders. Small berries (daphne, honeysuckle, red currant) in summer, and hips and haws pecked in winter. Large seeds (corn, sunflower, beech) opened by hammering. Will also take seed of trees (alder, birch, Scots pine.)

NESTING Builds in holes in trees and in a wide range of artificial structures—nest-boxes, letter-boxes, pumps, pipes, walls, electricity pylons, Nest mainly of moss with well-lined cup of hair and feathers. Clutch of about 8 eggs, white with variable amount of reddish spotting at big end; eggs usually covered by loose lining material until incubation begins.

Notes on The Great Tit

HAUNTS As for blue tit.

APPEARANCE Our largest tit. Other distinctive features are glossy black of head, nape and throat, completely surrounding white cheek-patch; black of throat continues in broad band (widening in male) down pale yellow breast and underparts.

VOICE Variable—some individuals can be recognised by voice. Calls include 'tsee-tsee' common to most tits, and a clinking note rather like 'pink' of chaffinch. Most typical song (from January onwards) a repeated disyllable 'tee-cher, tee-cher'; this, with its suggestion of the filing of metal, is the source of the nickname 'saw-sharpener'.

FOOD Very similar to that of blue tit, but greater power of bill widens range of food. Thus acorns, hard seeds of yew and oak-galls can be chipped open, or seeds hacked from runner bean pods or maize cobs. In mixed flocks foraging in woodland, tends to descend to ground more than other species.

NESTING Site as for blue tit, except that proportionately larger cavity and aperture needed, and that lining is of hair, wool or vegetable down without feathers. 6–10 eggs, like those of blue tit but larger and usually more heavily marked.

14. Blue Tit (above). Great Tit (below)

The Marsh Tit and the Coal Tit

The Marsh Tit Since this tit is less prone to make use of the facilities provided by the garden bird-table and nest-box, the general impression may be that it is a much less common bird than the ubiquitous blue and great tits; but in suitable areas it is exceedingly plentiful, and in woodland with undergrowth or thickets it may be the predominant tit species. In such areas it has a marked preference for the lower levels of tree and shrub growth, frequently descending to the ground to feed; in winter when flocks of mixed tits are scurrying through woodland from tree-tops to ground level, this stratification is most noticeable.

The marsh tit will readily accept unintentional provision of extra food, provided that it is offered in the correct surroundings; one of the best opportunities to observe this occurs when grain is being scattered on the woodland floor for the benefit of pheasants; at one such site the marsh tit population regularly demonstrated not only its surprisingly high numbers, but also that ability to learn and remember which seems a highly developed faculty in most tit species. At this particular site it was the custom of the game-keeper to announce feeding-time by a shrill soft whistling, and before the first pheasant had arrived, the trees were seething with marsh tits, each of which would descend to seize a single grain and then carry it off. In this forest one might have assumed that only a few pairs were present during the breeding-season, yet in late summer and early autumn the forestallers of the pheasants were estimated as between three and five hundred—and these apparently were only part of the total, for several other keepers were employing similar means of keeping their pheasant numbers together on their respective 'beats'.

Marsh tits may occur in damp, swampy thickets, but show no preference which would justify their misleading name. It is possible that another very similar species—the willow tit with almost identical plumage, but very different voice and habits—may have been the source of the error, for wet thickets with decaying willows are more typical of its nesting requirements. The recognition of the willow tit as a separate species dates only from the very end of the nineteenth century, and thus any earlier references to 'marsh tits' may refer to either species; certainly the 'marsh tit', recorded by the Victorian naturalist as excavating its nest-hole and carrying away the chips, was behaving in typical willow tit fashion.

The Coal Tit Apart from the very local crested tit of the Scottish Highlands, this is the tit most associated with coniferous woodland. In this preference it closely resembles the goldcrest, and just as the latter, in years when it is plentiful, will often be content with one large cedar or yew in an otherwise deciduous region, so may the coal tit take up residence in a garden or park with some specimens of fir, pine or cedar present. It may thus be a more frequent visitor to town garden bird-tables, since both in parks and older suburban gardens well-established conifers are often present, than in village or country gardens lacking these coal tit amenities. In another respect it resembles the goldcrest, for its high-pitched call may sometimes be run into a rapid trill not unlike that of its even smaller neighbour. In some respects also it is suggestive of the tree creeper, for it will often explore the bark on pine-trunks by a creeping, spiral ascent.

The ever-growing acreage of coniferous forests in Britain suits the coal tit in all but one respect—lack of nesting-holes in the sound young timber; but the resourceful coal tit (where nest-boxes are not provided) will make do with a ground-floor cranny among the buttress-roots of a tree.

Notes on The Marsh Tit

HAUNTS   Woodland, particularly deciduous with some bushy undergrowth.

APPEARANCE   About same size as blue tit, but appears slimmer; plumage dull-brown above, paler below, with no conspicuous features except glossy black of cap, extending to nape and just beneath chin, and whitish patch on cheek.

VOICE   Typical call (important as distinction between it and willow tit) usually of two notes, the first of which has peculiar 'spitting' quality—'pitchew'; also uses the 'see-see-see' call common to most tits. Song a repetition of notes 'chip-chip-chip' or 'chipee-chipee-chipee', sometimes becoming almost liquid trill.

FOOD   Mainly insects, but also seeds, including beechmast, sunflower or (when available) grain—hard seeds such as these carried up to perch and hammered; very fond of berries and, confusingly, may come to gardens when honeysuckle berries are ripe just as blackcap does.

NESTING   Usually in natural holes in trees, particularly those with very small entrances; may use crevices in walls, especially drystone-walling against a bank, as in a 'ha-ha' ditch. Nest mainly of moss, with thick layer of hair, wool or rabbit-fur on top. 6–8 eggs, white, thinly spotted with reddish-brown. Surprisingly loud, snake-like hissing from sitting bird if disturbed.

Notes on The Coal Tit

HAUNTS   See main text.

APPEARANCE   Slightly smaller than blue tit. Most distinctive feature is white nape dividing black of head from base of crown downwards. General plumage pattern very similar to that of blue tit, except that black replaces blue on and around head, and brownish-grey instead of blue on back and tail, while underparts are dull buff instead of yellow.

VOICE   In addition to common tit call, has a more musical call ending in a rapid twitter—'swee-tit-tit-tit'. Song very much like a less harsh version of great tit's 'tee-cher' song.

FOOD   Very much as for marsh tit, except that insect portion will be preponderantly of species found on conifers, including many forestry pests—larvae of moths, beetles and sawflies, and aphids. Will take large seeds and deal with them as marsh tit does; seeds from cones normally obtained when scales open in dry weather. All tits tend to hide or bury surplus seeds, and this species frequently observed to do so—sunflower seeds in tree crevices and beechmast in mossy turf.

NESTING   Very much as for marsh tit, except that tree-holes used are usually much lower, often near ground, and that holes in ground, bank, wall or rockery are commonly used. Both nest and eggs very similar to those of marsh tit.

15. Coal Tit (above). Marsh Tit (below)

The Long-tailed Tit

This miniature bird, whose tiny body carries such a disproportionate tail, would still be outstanding even if it were always common. It, like the goldcrest, is one of those border-line residents whose small mass can just endure a normal British winter, but which, in prolonged cold spells, gets reduced almost to the brink of extermination. Thanks to the security afforded by highly efficient nests, and the large size of families, the survivors of such catastrophes and their offspring, after a succession of mild or average winters, soon build up a reasonable population once again. But even when watching a party of thirty or forty scurrying through the orchard twigs, the knowledgeable observer, recalling the lean years, will still have the feeling that he is being favoured by a comparatively rare spectacle.

Whether called long-tailed tit or bottle tit, this is a tit in name only, for it belongs to a distinct sub-family of the true titmice. Although typically tit-like in acrobatic, hurried, but industrious searching of twigs and buds, and in sociability once breeding is over, the greatest contrast between this bird and the other tits is in their nesting methods. Whereas the tits proper merely stuff some convenient cavity with an untidy mass of material in which they form a cosy lined cup, the long-tailed tit not only constructs a nest in the open, but also can be said to be the master-craftsman among British nest-builders. The nests, whether in hawthorn, gorse, bramble or spruce, are remarkably standardised in size, shape and material. The outer covering is invariably a 'rough-cast plaster' of greyish lichen. Among hawthorn twigs shaggy with the same material this is good camouflage, but it can have the opposite effect against a dark green background of spruce or gorse needles. The explanation seems to be that the ancestral nesting-site of this species was the crutch of a lichened forest tree, and while this is still the traditional site for Scandinavian long-tailed tits, our British race has pioneered new ground by moving out into the twigs, but has omitted to adjust its materials to different surroundings. (Recent research has in fact shown that many of our birds do still nest in such situations—that they have been overlooked in the past is a testimonial to the success of the ancient mode of concealment.)

Although not shy when approached as they forage, long-tailed tits have not yet learned that sustenance may be found around human dwellings. There are a few recorded instances of this bird taking food from a bird-table in very severe weather; but strictly arboreal feeding habits—exploring twigs and buds, not descending to take food from the ground as other tits will—make it unlikely that this will ever become a common practice. (But note that, in times of emergency, artificial feeding is not impossible, though it is somewhat laborious: during the winter of 1962–63 a small party came regularly to feed from fruit-spurs which had been smeared with soft fat and then dusted with finely ground cheese.)

Notes on The Long-tailed Tit

HAUNTS   Hedgerows, gorsy commons, woodland edges, early stages of coniferous plantations; after leaf-fall denser woodland, coppices and orchards.

APPEARANCE   In silhouette, small size, very long tail and tit-like behaviour sufficient for identification. At closer quarters, most striking colour features are pink on back, shoulders, and flanks; white crown; mainly black wing and tail—latter with white outer edge, and markedly graduated. Striking close-up feature is apparently red, jewel-like eye; this is illusion created by 'spectacles' and eyebrow of pale red surrounding hazel-brown iris.

VOICE   Two very typical components are a rapid, trilling 'syrup', and a staccato purring 'prrup'; also typical tit 'tsee-tsee-tsee', but higher-pitched and more continuous than that of others.

FOOD   Minute insects such as aphids; eggs, larvae and pupae of small moths; spiders.

NESTING   May be only few feet off ground in bramble or gorse, but often much higher in trees. Nest almost size of coconut, but narrower. Completely domed like that of wren, but entrance hole nearer top; invariably symmetrically egg-shaped, with tight, clean outline. Basically of tightly felted moss with some cobweb, fragments of lichen plastered on outside, and tremendous quantity of soft feathers as lining. Building may take a fortnight, beginning in March, both birds sharing labour. Clutch of 8–12 pinkish-white eggs, with variable amount of reddish freckling, usually completed by mid-April.

The Goldcrest and the Spotted Flycatcher

The Goldcrest This has the distinction of being the smallest British bird, and its miniature proportions, coupled with its fondness for foraging high up in the foliage of conifers, makes it a bird whose presence is more often detected by ear than by eye. Its call, a repetitive thin, faint squeak, is so high-pitched that it is just at the limit of audibility for the human ear, and in fact ceases to be heard by many people at an age long before any general deterioration of hearing sets in. Once the call is known, a little patient watching is usually rewarded by at least a fleeting glimpse of the bird, for when its explorations have led it to the outer tip of a branch it will often hover in search of food, and indeed will often emerge to make flycatcher-like sallies into the air in pursuit of small insects.

In Britain during the breeding season it is almost invariably associated with conifers, including yews, but in years when this species is abundant it may become a garden bird, even well away from coniferous areas, provided that one large tree, or a few smaller ones, of the right family are present. Thus a town garden with one large cedar, or a cemetery with a few pyramidal Irish yews, may become a goldcrest breeding habitat. In winter the tie with conifers may be relaxed, and goldcrests may be found accompanying parties of tits through hedges and deciduous woodland. At such times they may also visit such unlikely plants as curly kale and brussels sprouts, and being extremely trusting can often be viewed from within a few feet. Among these winter birds some may be winter-visitors from the Continent, for in spite of its tiny size there is a regular influx in autumn from across the North Sea.

On account of its extremely small mass the goldcrest is unable to withstand prolonged spells of intense cold, and after such winters its numbers may be sadly reduced. Even in hard times it rarely comes to the bird-table, but if it is known to be in the neighbourhood, a sprinkling of finely-grated cheese on the nearest conifer (the flat fronds of cypress are very suitable) is eagerly taken.

The Spotted Flycatcher This is one of the most eagerly-awaited and best-known of summer visitors, not on account of appearance, for there is nothing noteworthy about its rather dull plumage, but because the activity which gives it its name so often takes place in close proximity to human dwellings. Its arrival also provides the climax to the annual spring influx of migrants, for together with the swift it is the last of the common summer visitors to arrive, usually at the very end of April or early in May. Its hunched and short-legged stance on fence, post or dead twig almost suggests lethargy, but the moment any winged prey comes within range it swiftly launches itself in pursuit, captures the insect (often with an audible snap of the bill) and then returns to its perch to resume its watch.

No other British bird consistently obtains its food in the same manner; its scarcer woodland relative, the pied flycatcher, will indulge in aerial chases after insects, but more frequently makes feeding sallies from its perch to seize prey on the ground or from the foliage and bark of trees. Although often nesting on or near a dwelling, the flycatcher never seems to be completely at ease in the presence of humans, and will swoop around the ears of the person who ventures near the nest, uttering squeaks of an explosive quality which suggest that the defender is spitting defiance. Although the presence of most other garden birds is tolerated, it is noteworthy that a trespassing pied wagtail (which may feed like a flycatcher) is invariably chased off.

Notes on The Goldcrest

HAUNTS   Coniferous woods and plantations, or gardens and parks with conifers. In winter may wander in other types of woodland.

APPEARANCE   Minute size; pale brownish-green plumage with very noticeable double white wing-bar. Crest orange in male, yellow in female, in each case with black border; not always very conspicuous, except when partially erected in spring display.

VOICE   High-pitched 'zit-zit-zit', which have been described as 'needle-points of sound'; song an elaboration of this, ending with distinct, trilling flourish.

FOOD   Almost entirely insects, in all stages, and spiders.

NESTING   Nest unique among British birds—suspended immediately beneath foliage at tip of branch of conifer (spruce, yew and cedar most favoured). Nest a tightly compacted cup of moss and cobweb, well-lined with feathers. Up to 10 eggs, transparent whitish-pink, with small brown spots at big end. Usually in April and May, followed by second brood later.

Notes on The Spotted Flycatcher

HAUNTS   Open woodland, gardens, parks and riverside willows.

APPEARANCE   Greyish-brown above, whitish below, with few black streaks on breasts and head. Sexes alike; young paler, with dark edges to feathers causing spotted appearance which has given name to species. But best recognised by stance and feeding-habits.

VOICE   Usual call a thin 'zee', with an anxious quality reminiscent of food-call of young song thrush; alarm call like this, but interspersed with 'chuck-chuck' sounds. Hardly any true song, but at close quarters during mating period high, squeaky 'zip, zip, zree' notes form a definite pattern.

FOOD   Mainly insects taken on wing; large beetle or worm occasionally taken from ground. Will often feed at dusk, and then large prey, such as noctuid moths, may be hammered on ground or other hard surface. In some seasons, usually just before emigration in August, will eat berries—red currants, yew, honeysuckle—but in others may use berried spray as flycatching perch and appear oblivious of potential food.

NESTING   Commonest natural site probably against trunk of tree where there is some other support such as junction with dead or living branch, old ivy stems, or partial hollow in dead wood; crowns or crevices in pollard willows. Artificial sites follow same general requirements—ledge on wall or building, particularly if partly sheltered above; ledge or beam inside open shed; space between trained tree and wall, or between drainpipe and building. Nest usually well-formed cup of moss, fibres and cobwebs, lined with fine roots and hairs, but owing to restriction of cramped sites is rarely completely circular. 4–5 eggs, bluish-green with spots and blotches of reddish-brown. Often a second brood. Young, perhaps owing to highly specialised feeding skill which they must acquire, dependent on adults for about a fortnight after flying.

17. Spotted Flycatcher (above, left).
Goldcrest, female (above, right),
male (below)

The Chiffchaff, the Willow Warbler and the Whitethroat

The warbler family, of which these three are members, forms a very high proportion of the millions of immigrants which swarm into our country between mid-March and mid-May. None of them, apart from the male blackcap, has any striking features of plumage to make identification easy; but nevertheless (with one exception which will be noted later) species which are very similar in general appearance are easily separable by song alone. The time to begin learning both the song and the appearance of birds of this initially difficult group is as they arrive, and on the whole this takes place in a fairly regular and well-spaced sequence which is helpful, for by mid-May when most species will be present, confusion can arise when four or five kinds are singing at once.

The Chiffchaff This is the earliest of our warblers to arrive, and it is often widespread and plentiful (at least in the southern half of England) before the end of March. It sings wherever it stops to feed and rest, and often this may be in sites where it will not stay to nest—parks, town gardens, tall elms and perhaps most favoured of all, riverside willows and beds of sallow. Like the cuckoo, it is a bird whose presence is proclaimed more often by sound than by sight, and even when the source of its metronomic song (which would be considered monotonous but for its implications of spring) is discovered, it is often too high to reveal details of colouring to the unaided eye. But two points of behaviour, which are typical of this and other leaf-warblers (whose scientific name, which may be translated as 'leaf-inspectors', is more apt), are noticeable even at a distance—the fidgety and somewhat tit-like industry of the small bird as it searches the buds or the opening flowers of sallow and elm, and the fact that singing and food-seeking are not separate activities, as with blackbirds and thrushes, but alternate almost casually in the process of twig-foraging.

The Willow Warbler Apart from very minor differences in plumage, leg-colour and wing-shape, this bird so closely resembles the chiffchaff that a silent specimen can often cause indecision even among expert observers. But when the bird sings all doubt vanishes, for the willow warbler has a very definite arrangement of pleasant notes which constitute a true song. It normally arrives about a fortnight after the chiffchaff, so that any leaf-warbler seen in March is more likely to be the latter.

The Whitethroat The whitethroat belongs to a group of the warblers whose members are larger than the leaf-warblers, and therefore differ in habits; there is also a tendency in this group for males and females to be distinguishable by plumage differences, but this is very obvious only in the blackcap. The whitethroat's song, a somewhat wheezy performance, is made more conspicuous than it would otherwise be by the striking combination of song and aerial display which occur together.

Notes on The Chiffchaff

HAUNTS For breeding, open woodland with tangles of ground-cover, or hedges and shrubberies, with taller trees. Latter needed for singing, for after breeding, birds haunt lower vegetation, often in treeless surroundings.

APPEARANCE A slim, gracefully active little bird, brownish above and whitish beneath. Closer view reveals greenish tinge to brown, and buff smudging on underparts. Faint pale eyestripe. In 'winter' plumage, midsummer onwards, underparts become cleaner white.

VOICE Rhythmical repetition of pairs of notes, the first higher than the second—'chiff-chaff' or 'tweet-twat', varied by occasional introduction of third note—'chiff-chiff-chaff'. Mostly delivered from high in tree. During pauses between songs late in season, utters faint creaking notes, detectable, once known, at considerable range. Call a short, plaintively sweet 'hweet'.

FOOD Almost entirely insectivorous; will hover to take aphids from beneath leaf, and make aerial sallies to capture insects on wing.

NESTING Nest roughly like that of wren, but with wider side-entrance; somewhat untidy ball of dead leaves or bracken, moss and grass, concealed in ground-tangle, or in dense evergreens like box and yew; usually within three feet of ground, but often much higher in evergreens. Nest feather-lined; about 6 eggs, white with dark reddish spots.

Notes on The Willow Warbler

HAUNTS Can inhabit woodland alongside chiffchaff, but tall trees not essential; open scrub or bushy commons with areas of coarse grass, or hedgerows with rough basal vegetation.

APPEARANCE Like chiffchaff, but slightly longer, greener above and more yellow below; becomes brighter in winter plumage—birds of the year, frequent in July, appear almost canary yellow beneath.

VOICE A very regular pattern of about a dozen notes, beginning with faint, deliberate whistles, becoming faster and louder, then fading away in lower-pitched notes. Call much like chiffchaff's.

FOOD Very much as for chiffchaff, but berries regularly eaten in summer.

NESTING Nest domed like chiffchaff's, but since on ground in grass or herbage, an igloo rather than a ball; well-lined with feathers. About 6 eggs, usually less heavily marked than those of chiffchaff.

Notes on The Whitethroat

HAUNTS Open country with bushes or hedges. Normally forages close to ground. After breeding, common in gardens and field-crops.

APPEARANCE Separable from other small brownish birds by contrasting gingerish-brown of wings, and white beneath throat and on outer tail feathers. Male has grey cap, and faint pinkish flush on buff of underparts; females and juveniles lack these features.

VOICE Song a wheezy, rapid warble, undistinguished except when combined with bouncing dance above hedge-top. Call a grating 'kaarr' or a sharp 'tack-tack'.

FOOD Mainly insects, particularly caterpillars and aphids, but distinctly fond of some types of fruit.

NESTING Usually low in brambles, hedges or bushes. Nest built of roots and grass, with deep, well-made cup lined with hair. 4–5 eggs, very variable, commonly greenish-brown spotted and blotched with darker colours.

18. Chiffchaff (above).
Whitethroat, male (middle).
Willow Warbler (below)

The Blackcap and the Garden Warbler

The Blackcap   Great tits, coal tits, marsh tits, and even the misnamed black-headed gull, have in different localities all shared this name, so that earlier writers often insisted on calling this bird the 'blackcap warbler'. Such additional clarification is now superfluous, and the name nowadays is so well-established that it conjures up, not so much the colour of a head (which on the whole is seldom seen) but the sound of a voice, for it is as a songster that it is renowned. The song, which together with that of the willow warbler is among the most musical of sounds to be heard from newly arrived migrants in early April, is considered by some to be second only to that of the nightingale; others, fully aware of the rich, wild beauty of some warbled phrases, might say that it could be, if only the bird would sing more continuously. But, as with the garden warbler, there is a great deal of variation in the quality of song from bird to bird.

There are two periods in the year when the best opportunities for seeing this bird (for a great part of its stay hidden in foliage) occur; one is on its arrival in early April before the buds have fully opened; the other, often possible through a window and without the aid of binoculars, is in July and August when both adults and young will come into gardens and are particularly attracted to honeysuckle berries. But a word of caution is necessary here—the black-capped marsh tit is also very partial to the same fruit.

Blackcaps heard and seen in late March may be the vanguard of the main spring invasion, but on the other hand they may have been wintering birds. Whether this habit of staying in Britain is a newly acquired and rapidly increasing one, or whether the number of winter records is merely pro-portionate to the growth in numbers of competent observers, is uncertain. At first, sight-records were dismissed by sceptics as mistakenly identified marsh or willow tits—in spite of the fact that some of the records were of brown-headed females. Since then the matter has been put beyond doubt by the capture and precise identification of many winter specimens. (The most recent, within six yards of where this is being written, with different individuals on November 28th, 29th and 30th, and a fourth bird on December 23rd.) From the gap between the disappearance of the last summer visitors (usually in August) and the appearance of these winter birds (usually in November and December), there seems a distinct possibility that these are not left-overs from summer, but northern European birds using Britain instead of Mediterranean regions as winter-quarters.

The Garden Warbler   The blackcap is a typical member of the group of larger warblers which have, in the majority of species, dark caps and some differentiation between male and female plumage; the garden warbler, although a member of the same family, is an exception in this respect, for both sexes have plumage—brownish above, paler beneath—of an extremely sober pattern. Arriving later than the blackcap, and even more prone to take advantage of the leafy cover then available, its presence is more often detected by ear than by eye. If the blackcap is a melodious but somewhat temperamental soprano, the garden warbler is a placid and earnest contralto, for its rich, throaty warblings are long-sustained and lack the staccato quality, and all-too-brief staying-power, of the blackcap's performance; to be fair to the latter, its song is becoming thin and past its best by the time that side-by-side comparisons are possible; but to many ears (or possibly temperaments) the song of a good (prima donna) garden warbler is the more satisfactory. In spite of the blackcap's proven ability to withstand a British winter, it is mainly plentiful in the south, whereas the garden warbler is much more widely distributed.

Notes on The Blackcap

HAUNTS For breeding, open woodland with bushy undergrowth, old hedges with suitable brambly bottoms, or parks and large gardens with similar mixture of trees and bushy ground-cover. Frequent in gardens in post-breeding dispersal.

APPEARANCE Male, apart from glossy black cap (on crown only, not extending to nape as in much smaller marsh tit), distinctly greyish-brown, grey most noticeable around head and on wings; underparts greyish-white. Female same pattern as male, but cap is of bright reddish-brown, and other parts browner, not greyish. Young very like female, except that in early stages cap is paler, and less well demarcated. Before departure brown cap is already deepening in some young males.

VOICE Scolding call (frequent when parents and broods are still roaming together) a harsh 'tack-tack'. Song a clear, rather high-pitched warbling, often with fluting notes reminiscent of blackbird, typically increasing in volume towards finish.

FOOD Insects mainly, but also markedly fond of small succulent fruit—raspberries, currants, honeysuckle, elder, daphne—in summer; wintering birds (1964) all feeding on apples still on tree.

NESTING Sometimes very near ground, in brambles, dewberry, or even rank nettles and hogweed, but more often higher in hedge or dense bush. Nest a frail structure of fibres and grass stems, but invariably well-tethered to supporting twigs; lined with finer fibres, sometimes hair. 4–5 eggs, buffish with darker brown blotches, but very variable.

Notes on The Garden Warbler

HAUNTS Very much as for blackcap, and often both species found together, but at least some trees seem essential for latter, and garden warbler may be found in sufficiently bushy areas without trees. In spite of name, less frequent in gardens than any of the common warblers.

APPEARANCE No distinctive features—a brownish bird with paler underparts.

VOICE The main distinguishing feature, but nevertheless sight of bird advisable before deciding whether this species or blackcap responsible. Apart from such evidence, helpful distinguishing features are later song-period (late May and throughout June), more sustained and even warbling, lacking final loud burst, and general lower, more throaty quality. 'Tacking' call like blackcap's.

FOOD Very similar to that of blackcap, including fondness for fruit.

NESTING Similar sites to low-building blackcaps. Nest somewhat bulkier, but not usually interwoven with supporting stems. 4–5 eggs, variable, but usually dirty yellowish or greenish with darker spots and blotches.

19. Blackcap, male (above, right), female (above, left). Garden Warbler (below)

The Redwing and the Fieldfare

Many of our winter visitors, from mallards to starlings and chaffinches, may arrive unnoticed, except that the experienced observer may deduce what has happened from a sudden increase in local numbers. This is because, for all practical purposes, they are identical in plumage and habits with residents of the same species. But with the arrival of these two distinctive winter thrushes, which do not breed here (apart from a few redwings which now nest in Scotland), there can be no doubt that winter immigration has taken place. Since they are usually in flocks, whether feeding or in transit, and have easily recognised calls, their passage or arrival is seldom overlooked.

The Redwing   The overhead sound of 'wild birds that change their season in a night, and wail their way from cloud to cloud' is one of the most thrilling and somewhat eerie phenomena of bird-life. Tennyson, one assumes, was referring to the noisy nocturnal calls of waders keeping flock-contact in the darkness, but if 'sigh' were substituted for 'wail', the quotation would fit an unseen passage of redwings. The flight-call, usually heard for the first time on some dark night in October or November, is a faint 'see' or 'seep', and may be heard at intervals of seconds or minutes, presumably in proportion to the density and extent of the unseen flock. But although the call is faint, it is penetrating, and the practised ear can sometimes detect it through the hubbub of city traffic.

Often at first light on the morning after this first intimation of the presence of redwings has been noticed, small parties may still be seen going over, and often one will discover that some are foraging in the fields or hedges. At this time of the year parties of birds, which look like song thrushes, both in size and general coloration, are worth a closer inspection. The first clue is the very fact of congregation, for song thrushes rarely gather in parties. In spite of the vision conjured up by the name, there is little red visible in a redwing perched among the haws or hopping in soft pastures. The most noticeable feature which distinguishes it from a song thrush on such occasions is a very distinct pale buff eyestripe. Once this has been noted the 'red' of the flanks, and in flight a greater exposure of the same colour (a rusty-orange) when the wing is raised, can clinch the identification.

Redwings are the most delicate of the larger thrushes, and are some of the first victims of hard winters; but they spread the risk by a very widespread westerly and southerly dispersal from their breeding-grounds in Scandinavia and Eastern Europe. Apparently they are not consistent in their choice of winter resorts, for a ringed bird recovered in Cyprus one winter had been marked as a winter-visitor to Britain in a previous winter.

The Fieldfare   This is much the larger of the two winter thrushes, being about equal in size to a mistle thrush. Although often mingling with redwings, blackbirds and song thrushes, particularly in hard weather when they are all feeding on berries, they tend to keep together in conditions of softer weather, when pure flocks, which may be of several hundred, quarter the ground in search of worms, slugs and small snails. These feeding assemblies exhibit a remarkable compromise between communal and territorial behaviour, for although they all move in one direction as a well-disciplined flock, each individual is spaced at about a yard from the next.

Winter residents of this species have regular roosts, sometimes in coarse grassland or ground vegetation, but often in scrub or tall hedges. The morning and afternoon flights, punctuated by the harsh 'oo-chack-chack' contact calls, then become a familiar part of the winter scene.

Notes on The Redwing

HAUNTS   Open fields with short grass—pastures, valley or downland, playing-fields—favoured in mild weather. Resorts to hedges, open woodland, scrub, or wherever berries may be found when ground frozen or snow-covered. Roosts in evergreen shrubberies, thickets such as mature coppice, or in thick overgrown hedges.

APPEARANCE   Could pass for song thrush at casual glance; separable by distinct eye-stripe, reddish flush on flanks, and more of same orange-brown revealed beneath lifted wing.

VOICE   Call-note described in main text. At roost this is often mingled with distinct 'chisick' call. At roosting assemblies also, especially towards end of stay—late March or early April—beginnings of song may be heard in chorus, a pleasant mixture of twittering and piping 'twee' call.

FOOD   From ground, worms, leather-jackets, insect larvae and pupae, beetles and snails—latter small species swallowed whole; has not song thrush's ability to deal with larger species. From trees and shrubs, berries of hawthorn, rowan, rose, yew, holly and juniper.

NESTING   Cannot be classed as regular breeder in Britain, except for a few pairs in one locality in Scottish Highlands.

Notes on The Fieldfare

HAUNTS   Very similar to those of redwing, with which it often associates; flocks (often mingled with lapwings and gulls) attracted to partially-flooded meadows, or fields from which floods have just subsided. In very hard weather, flocks may break up, and individuals will then occupy temporary territories in gardens if berries or fallen apples available; such individualists very aggressive, driving off both starlings and blackbirds.

APPEARANCE   Resembles mistle thrush in size and stance, also in having speckled breast and silvery-white undersides to wings; but from rear striking colour pattern at once separates it—pigeon-grey head and rump, chestnut-brown back and almost black tail. In some lights pale rump, against contrasting black tail, may appear almost white. Very vocal and gregarious. Flocks both on ground and in flight typically in very open formation.

VOICE   Usual call a harsh, guttural 'oo-chack-chack'; also, particularly when foraging in berried trees and bushes, a soft 'see' call, something like that of redwing but more drawn out. In roosts towards end of stay (April or even early May) chorus of feeble wheezy chuckles and whistles may be heard— probably forerunner of true song.

FOOD   Very similar to that of redwing, but perhaps more regular feeder on berries; more powerful bill can also tackle harder fare, such as swedes, in time of food shortage.

NESTING   Not a British breeder—returns to nest in Europe, from northern Scandinavia to Switzerland and eastward.

20   Redwing (above and middle).
Fieldfare (below)

The Song Thrush and the Mistle Thrush

The Song Thrush This is one of the most familiar and popular British birds, for a great variety of reasons. In the first place it is a frequenter of gardens, where its comparatively large size and speckled breast make it easily recognisable; there also it indulges in spectacular feeding-behaviour which at once sets it apart as a special bird, for its use of an anvil-stone upon which to smash snails is an almost unique example of regular tool-using by a native bird, only equalled by the vice-using nuthatch; but above all it is the earliest true songster of the year, and moreover sings in a fairly regular pattern to which words may be fitted. Even before Browning immortalised its habit of singing each song twice over, well-established word-versions beginning with twice-repeated phrases such as 'Pretty Dick, pretty Dick' had already noted this typical habit. An added attraction is the plaster-lined nest which cannot be mistaken for that of any other bird, and the invariable and beautiful eggs which it holds.

Although almost as fond of fruit as the blackbird, it is never regarded as anything but a desirable bird in the garden, safeguarded by its proven worth as a seeker-out and destroyer of snails. It is also useful in the garden in a less obvious way, for strange as it may seem for a bird of its size, it will gather aphids from infested fruit-trees or roses. Compared with the other common member of the thrush family, the blackbird, the song thrush is less adaptable in finding food in hard winters, and frequently its numbers are much reduced following a prolonged hard spell. A certain proportion of our native birds avoid this threat by autumn movement to the milder south-west, not infrequently crossing the channel to France, particularly Brittany.

The Mistle Thrush The possession of a variety of local or vernacular names, dating back to long before the deliberate coinings of names by early naturalists, is a sure indication that the possessor had some quality worthy of notice—appearance, habits, edibility or voice. In the case of the mistle thrush the accepted name refers to one characteristic, a partiality to mistletoe-berries; but most other names— storm-cock, thrice-thrush and screech-thrush—derive from aspects of vocal behaviour. The far-reaching whistle of the mistle thrush may be heard in any sort of weather between Christmas and May, but its habit of singing defiantly, when wind or foul weather have silenced all other competitors, cause the brief song-phrase to be better known than it would be but for this solo performance. The usual triple grouping of notes must be the origin of 'thrice-thrush', while the 'screech' refers to another outstanding characteristic—a noisy aggressiveness towards rivals, cats or human intruders.

Although size alone distinguishes this bird from the song thrush, another marked difference is in the sociability of the mistle thrush immediately the breeding season is over. At first family parties of five or six, later joining to form flocks of from thirty to forty, roam the countryside. Although this species is associated with high trees when singing or nesting, the wandering flocks of summer and autumn may be met with on downland, moors and even bog. But the mistle thrush is an early nester and by midwinter not parties, but pairs, will be found at night in the ivy-clumps which are one of its favourite roosting-sites.

Notes on The Song Thrush

HAUNTS Open woodland with undergrowth, hedges, bushy commons, scrub, parks and gardens.

APPEARANCE Smaller size, browner back, warm buff background to speckled breast, orange-buff underwing, and lack of whitish outer tail-feathers, all distinguish from mistle thrush; redwing most alike in size and general coloration, but latter has prominent pale eye-stripe, reddish flush on flanks, and redder underwing—latter also more sociable.

VOICE Usually delivered from perch high on tree or building; clear and musical, but without fluting quality of blackbird; usually in short phrases of three or four notes, repeated three or four times, interspersed with longer notes, also usually repeated a few times before continuing with faster notes. Call a faint 'sip'.

FOOD Snails and earthworms chief diet from ground, also insect larvae from both ground and foliage. Wide variety of fruit and berries eaten.

NESTING Usually at no great height in bush or hedge; nest of dead grass and root-fibres, or moss, compacted with damp earth, but unique feature is lining cup of cardboard-like plaster made from rotten wood, dung and saliva; 4–5 eggs, slightly greener than sky-blue, spotted with black.

Notes on The Mistle Thrush

HAUNTS Woods, coniferous plantations, gardens or parks with large trees; more open country in summer and autumn.

APPEARANCE Differs from song thrush in much greater size; uniform greyish-brown of back; heavy speckling on whiter breast; whitish outer tail-feathers; and dipping, woodpecker-like flight. Young have pale heads and light-mottled, scaly plumage.

VOICE Short phrases of three or four notes, almost as mellow as fluting of blackbird, but shriller and wilder, with intonation which suggests that a question is being asked. Call a harsh 'chee-er'.

NESTING Often begins in February; site usually a fork high in tree. Nest similar to song thrush's, but lacking plaster lining. 4–5 eggs, typically bluish with reddish spots and blotches.

21. Mistle Thrush (above).
Song Thrush (below)

The Blackbird

This is undoubtedly our most plentiful breeding species of land bird, and although its fine song is limited to a comparatively short season, at all other times it continues to give audible notice of its presence, for it is one of the chief alarmists of garden, hedgerow and woodland; also, during winter, it is as noisy as the pheasant in advertising the fact that it is going to roost. Although not a sociable species in the same way as redwings and fieldfares, roosting assemblies of from twenty to a hundred birds are quite usual, and the amount of chasing and rivalry exhibited before the flock settles down, and the preponderance of males, suggests that this is a pre-mating ritual rather than a mere roosting assembly. Usually at the early morning dispersal from such a roost, blackbirds may be seen feeding in what may be regarded as a very widely-spaced flock, and another characteristic—that of never venturing far from the cover of hedge or trees—may then be noted.

Blackbirds and song thrushes, the two commonest medium-sized birds of garden and hedgerow, share many food-gathering activities—searching lawns and meadows for earthworms, following the gardener's spade or fork for worms or grubs, and pecking fruit and eating berries. But in spite of the song thrush's superiority in the matter of making use of snails, the blackbird is the better adapted of the two when it comes to procuring food in hard times. Its greater bulk certainly gives it some slight advantage in resisting extreme cold, but the more important factor in helping it to survive is its digging and scuffling technique which enables it to find food beneath leaf-litter when none is available on the surface; evidence of this strength of feet is not confined to the tell-tale debris on the snow at the hedge-bottom—the gardener's mulch of humus may be similarly scattered during a droughty summer.

The distinctive plumage of the cock blackbird makes it an unmistakable bird, but the same cannot be said of females and young; for such a common garden-nesting species, it is amazing how frequently the brown hen leads people to conclude (and report) that a mixed marriage has taken place between a thrush and a blackbird. The first-year male, changing from juvenile to adult plumage from early August onward, can look very odd in a parti-coloured coat containing large patches of both the new black and the old mottled brown.

In spite of its ability to cope with hard weather, the blackbird is not entirely a static resident; some portion of our population moves, usually to milder western areas and Eire, at the approach of winter, and our winter numbers are considerably augmented by immigrants from across the North Sea. Since these European birds (unlike Continental song thrushes) are indistinguishable from our native birds in plumage or behaviour, their arrival is not so obvious as that of the fieldfare and redwing; but, often coinciding with the arrival of the last two species, sudden increases in blackbird numbers may be noted—and at night the 'sip' flight-call may be heard. The recovery of marked birds suggests that the countries around the Baltic are the breeding-haunts of these winter immigrants.

Notes on The Blackbird

HAUNTS   Extremely varied—from gardens and woodland to practically treeless moorland and islands.

APPEARANCE   All black plumage of adult male, with orange bill and eye-rim, unmistakable; first-winter cock lacks orange adornments, but these may be seen appearing in various stages throughout winter; female dull brown above; redder brown underparts, lighter at throat and below breast, all flecked and mottled with darker brown, and tail brownish-black. (Some females have greyer underparts.) Young very similar to female, but paler and redder above, and more distinctly speckled below.

VOICE   Common call at slight disturbance is a subdued 'chook-chook'; real alarm expressed by rapid utterance of this call succeeded by screeching notes—'chook-chook-chook—askree, skree, skree.' Pre-roosting call (or mobbing call around owl or cat) a monotonous 'pit-pit'. Most remarkable feature of song is clear, fluting whistle, delivered in an effortless—almost offhand—manner, repeated once or twice and ending with short warble; but extremely variable, and many individuals have lilting opening themes which identify them; these may not infrequently be based on calls of other birds, from redshank to stone curlew.

FOOD   Animal matter mainly obtained from ground—worms, grubs, small snails (eaten whole), but caterpillars may be gathered from foliage when rearing young; vegetable matter, in addition to almost any garden fruit or wild berry, includes seeds; in hard weather, will peck at swedes, and (personal observation) strongly suspected of excavating around wild arum to peck at corm.

NESTING   Very adaptable as to site—normally fairly low in bush or tree, often in or on buildings, and quite often on ground of bank or edge of ditch. Nest perhaps more variable externally than that of song thrush and often bulkier—moss, dead grass or straw, dead leaves, paper, with core of muddy earth; cup lined with mud, on which final lining of dry grass is placed. Usually 5 eggs, basically blue-green with reddish spots or markings, but latter may vary from heavy minute uniform spotting resulting in almost khaki-brown effect, to few larger but sparser markings.

22. Blackbird, male (above),
female (below)

The Dunnock and the Robin

The Dunnock   Before the days of scientific classification, the implications contained in the everyday names of many birds and animals were of little importance; a nightjar could be a fern owl, a tern a sea swallow, a willow warbler a willow wren, and a bat a flittermouse. Nowadays, when it is felt that such names suggest family affinities which do not exist, most of them have been found unacceptable for general usage, although they are still of interest as vernacular nicknames. But for some reason the dunnock is still stubbornly called a hedge sparrow by people who know perfectly well that it is no kind of sparrow. The argument that 'the name that was good enough for Shakespeare is good enough for me' might be extended to the acceptance of the semi-magical natural history recorded by the same authoritative pen. Even in precedence of known usage 'dunnock' (A.D. 1475) has priority over 'hedge sparrow' (A.D. 1530). But apart from this controversial matter of naming or mis-naming, the dunnock arouses little interest as it shuffles around our gardens and parks. It comes into its own at last when its early nest is found, for the brilliance of its bright blue eggs is the one conspicuous feature in the life of this bird.

But for all its lack of any outstanding qualities, the sober little dunnock, for no very obvious reasons, is a remarkably plentiful and successful species. It resembles the wren in its adaptability to widely differing surroundings, and is just as much at home on some bleak, heathery moorland or gale-swept Hebridean island, as around the door in a suburban garden. Its size and ability to subsist on seeds when animal matter is scarce render it less susceptible than the wren to severe winters. When cuckoos were more plentiful they must have been effective natural regulators of dunnock population, for this bird is much favoured as a foster-parent for the young cuckoo. Now, with both cuckoos and hawks much scarcer than they once were, the dunnock has few enemies except cats—or people who still think it may be destroyed as a 'sparrow'.

The Robin   Flowers as national emblems have been in vogue for many centuries, but it is only in recent years that the idea of a national bird for each country has come into fashion. When British public opinion was assessed by letters to the Press, the robin easily topped the poll. But the answer was already available without any such testing, for the robin had long ago established its position by the unique character of its name. Tom Tit, Jenny Wren, Jack Daw and Mag Pie all carry some suggestion of human interest and affection, but Robin (Redbreast) is the only one whose 'Christian' name is sufficient by itself. The robin itself might put the matter the other way round and say that it chose the British people, for the affinity which the robin shows for human society is a peculiarity of the British race—Continental robins are mainly shy forest-dwellers, and other species take over the duties of crumb-gleaner and assistant gardener performed by the British robin.

In other respects also the robin is unique, for not only do both cock and hen sing, but they do so almost the whole year round, apart from a short lull in July. Both cock and hen also, after the summer moult, occupy individual territories, from which they warn off others of their kind by song (often at its best in autumn), fights and chases. This territorial pugnacity, following soon after the maturity of the young, is undoubtedly the basis of the old fable that young robins kill off the old ones each year. But even without such drastic measures, a robin's expectation of life is short—probably around one and a half years. Few apparently die of old age (the occasional known five-year-old is as spry as ever), but the robin is accident-prone and a violent death from car, cat, mouse-trap or motor-mower is a common end. It has been suggested that the very boldness and inquisitiveness of the robin leads it to take risks, even with cats and machinery.

Notes on The Dunnock

HAUNTS   Very varied, but more associated with bushes and low vegetation than with trees, and needs certain amounts of clear ground between—hence common in parks and gardens.

APPEARANCE   A sparrow-sized brownish bird, but with pointed slender bill which at once serves to separate it from seed-eating sparrow. Head, neck and throat mainly soft blue-grey, browner on crown and cheeks; upper parts reddish-brown, streaked darker. Rather loose plumage gives plump appearance, and shuffling run creates impression of short legs—latter appear normal when fully-extended for hopping.

VOICE   A feeble 'sweedle-deedle-deedle', almost unnoticed among general clamour of late spring, but very pleasant in isolation of winter, for song may be heard all the year round. Call a relatively powerful, piping squeak.

FOOD   Mainly insects and other small animal life in summer, but also fond of succulent berries such as red-currants. In winter, whatever animal food is available, supplemented by small weed-seeds.

NESTING   Nest, usually in thick hedge or bush, mainly of moss with few small twigs and fibres; very solidly made, and deep cup lined with hair, wool or few feathers; about 5 eggs, of striking bright blue.

Notes on The Robin

HAUNTS   Requirements—patches of open ground with presence of tree or bush-cover—provided by wide range of environments, from natural woodland to gardens, parks and cemeteries.

APPEARANCE   Orange-red breast and forehead unmistakable; sexes alike; before early-autumn assumption of adult plumage, young, with speckled buff breasts and scaly back plumage, are not 'redbreasts', but still recognisably robins from typical stance and behaviour.

VOICE   A liquid, rather shrill warble, to some ears melancholy rather than cheerful; both sexes sing, often from cover, sometimes from prominent perch on tree or building.

FOOD   Mainly insects, particularly 'grubs'; also earthworms, spiders, centipedes. In summer most small succulent berries, wild and cultivated, as important supplementary diet.

NESTING   Favoured natural sites are steep banks with overhead shelter, hollow trees, or beneath exposed roots in river-bank. Artificial sites (much used) include discarded tins and kettles, ledges in sheds, and not infrequently within house or busy workshop itself.

23. Robin (above). Dunnock (below)

The Wren

The wren is almost certainly the most widely distributed species of bird in Britain, for whereas almost every other species is limited by more or less well-defined requirements such as woodland, moorland, open grassland, fens, sea-shore or reed-beds, the wren can exist successfully in any of these varied environments. It can be said to inhabit and exploit not any one type of habitat, but rather the bottom-most layer—the ground itself and a few feet above it—of them all. This zone, at the base of covering vegetation, is rich in insects, spiders and other minute forms of animal life, and among birds the wren has sole hunting-rights here. The dunnock shows some inclination to exploit similar zones, but its size limits its scope, and it is barred from dense tangles through which the wren threads its way as easily as a mouse. It is not only dark vegetation which it explores, and one need not go as far as a boulder-strewn shore in the Shetlands or Hebrides to have proof of the wren's fearless exploration of dark crannies and passages through rocks—in timber-yards, coal-stacks and builders' yards one can observe spider-hunting wrens disappearing into one cranny and eventually emerging from another, sometimes many yards away. The zone next to the earth's surface referred to does not necessarily have to be horizontal—near-vertical sea-cliffs, with crannies and overhanging tufts of vegetation, or even the sea-weed itself at low tide, will still provide the requisite habitat.

For this very specialised mode of life the wren is admirably adapted—tiny body, but with comparatively stout legs and large probing beak; but its very smallness is the one chink in its armour. The wren, like the goldcrest, is dogged by the mathematical fact that surface area of a sphere increases in inverse ratio with its diameter—in other words, the smaller the bird the greater (proportionately) the surface from which body-heat can be lost. Thus the wren was one of the most severely reduced of common species in the prolonged hard winter of 1962–63. In a garden where annual records of birds passing through is kept, there were 91 known individuals in 1961; in 1962, following a winter in which there had been a short period of intense cold, the number had dropped to 60; after the worst winter of all, the number had fallen to six; but providing that a breeding nucleus is left, the wren soon recovers from such approaches to the brink of extermination; it is pleasant to record that the total for 1964 was 23.

The wren takes what steps it can to avoid loss of heat in the long winter nights; for instead of roosting in bushes in the open, as it will do in milder weather, it seeks a warm shelter such as a nest of its own kind, a house martin's nest, a nest-box, or it may squeeze its way into the side of a rick. In extreme cold (as if aware of the mathematical law) parties of from five to ten may huddle together in such snug shelters, thus effectively producing a larger spherical mass.

Notes on The Wren

HAUNTS Almost anywhere, provided that some traces of ground-cover are present—see main text.

APPEARANCE Apart from very small size, one of chief distinguishing features is plump stubbiness, accentuated both by shortness of tail and fact that latter is usually cocked over back. At close quarters plumage, which normally is seen as rufous above and paler beneath, shows delicate pattern of barring with darker shades, particularly on wings, tail and flanks. Distinct pale buff eyestripe. Bustling activity and whirring of wings in short flights, both typically not far above ground, also distinguish wren from our other diminutive species, the goldcrest.

VOICE Typical call is rapidly repeated ticking sound with a vibrant quality. Song, which may be heard all the year round, is remarkably powerful considering small organ which produces it—effect on human ear-drum at range of few feet can be almost shattering; it begins with a few separate high-pitched notes, rapidly accelerates, and finishes by putting all its energy into the final explosive trill.

FOOD In addition to small animal life from near ground, will visit bushes and trees for caterpillars and aphids during rearing of young. Will occasionally eat small, succulent fruit, e.g. red-currants and honeysuckle berries.

NESTING Prefers sites that are sheltered, often in dim light—overhanging banks of ditches and rivers, ivy, clefts or hollows in trees, dense brambles, ledges inside barns and sheds. Nest more or less spherical mass of any handy material—moss, dead leaves, bracken—completely domed with entrance at side. Cock builds several nests, but lining with feathers is done by hen when nest chosen. 5–8 eggs, white with dark reddish spots.

24. Wren

The Swift and the Swallow

The Swift From its roughly similar shape and habits, the swift was classed by early naturalists as a species of swallow, but structurally it belongs to a totally different group, that containing the humming-birds. The swift needs solid support beneath for one function only—nesting; otherwise it can feed, drink, gather nesting-materials, mate and even sleep while still airborne. But the air in which it spends so much of its life must be sufficiently warm and calm for insects to be on the wing, and in sudden cold, wet spells the swift may lie up in a semi-dormant state. Young in the nest are protected against such foodless spells by an ability to assume a state approaching the cold-blooded torpor of hibernating animals.

The fact that it is normally observed on the wing, and never walking, hopping or perching, coupled with the fact that its legs and feet are very short, led to the ancient belief that a swift was footless— a myth perpetuated both in the meaning of its scientific name and also in the armorial swift, which is the footless 'martlet' of heraldry. The swift's stay is short for a summer migrant—the three months from early May to early August, a period coinciding with high insect population and long hours of daylight. Even when summer, judged by the thermometer, seems only just getting under way, the swift has no reason for staying to enjoy it, once its young can fly. There seems no need for the young to strengthen their wings by a period of practice-flights; it is known that a young bird can be hundreds of miles southwards on its first trip to African winter-quarters within two days of its first 'launching'. Swifts, for their size, are long-lived, for individuals known to be nineteen and fifteen years old are on record; and these died, not of old-age, but from accidental causes—including collision at speed with another swift.

The Swallow Just as the call of the cuckoo is the most welcome and widely recognised sound of spring, so is the sight of the first swallow, its visual counterpart, for it is the first migrant likely to be seen by those who do not deliberately set out to meet each returning species as its time becomes due. Its house-haunting habits, and particularly its faithfulness to old sites, combined with distinctive plumage and a musical twitter, make its arrival difficult to miss. The returning birds appear to have a remarkable sense of exact location; thus when an old shed was replaced, during winter, by a modern structure, the former swallow tenant, on the day of its arrival, repeatedly swooped and hovered at the blank new wall, at the precise spot where formerly the ever-open half-door had been.

The swallow, before the days of settled human communities, must have been restricted to areas in which caves or hollow trees afforded nesting-sites. Even when the widespread substitution of chimney pots for wide open chimneys put an end to one traditional nesting-site, the ex-'chimney-swallow' had still many alternatives in both town and country—stables, coach-houses, cowsheds, pig-sties and outhouses—in which to nest. Modern methods of housing both the current form of 'horse-power' and farm livestock leave fewer points of access for the home-seeking swallow today, and there is a general impression that the species is not now so plentiful as it once was. But, however true this may be of an observer's immediate surroundings, the large southward passages throughout September and early October, and the vast roosting-assemblies in reed-beds in the same period, supply reassuring evidence that somewhere the swallow still breeds in abundance.

Notes on The Swift

HAUNTS Anywhere between ground-level and several hundred feet above—far-ranging feeding and weather-avoiding flights make it liable to be seen over any kind of country. For breeding, though occasionally natural crag or cliff-crevices are used, greatest concentrations are where buildings offer nesting-niches—hence particularly plentiful in old cities, towns and villages.

APPEARANCE Separable from swallow by apparently all-black plumage (actually sooty-brown with whitish throat); longer and narrower scythe-blade wings; short tail, only slightly forked; and more entirely aerial habits.

VOICE Commonest utterance is the flight-call, a prolonged 'quee' or 'squee', much used in chasing parties.

FOOD Entirely insects taken on the wing.

NESTING Dark crannies or cavities in tiles, thatch, masonry or natural sites. Nest composed of suitable matter seized in flight—feathers, straws, paper, dead leaves—formed into shallow cup by addition of gelatinous saliva. 2–3 pure white eggs.

Notes on The Swallow

HAUNTS Open country with human habitations and outbuildings, particularly if some water in neighbourhood.

APPEARANCE Blue-black plumage of back, red-brown breast and forehead, and long forked tail at once distinguish this from others of swallow family.

VOICE A pleasant short twittering note much used in flight, but song from perch, or sometimes in flight, a musical, warbling mixture of 'tweetzee' sounds.

FOOD Insects, from small gnats to crane-flies, taken on wing; in exceptional cases may take food from ground—large party, probably passage-migrants, once observed settled on sea-shore, making short runs to capture sand-hoppers.

NESTING Usually within building, and most often in position with some support beneath, such as on rafter or in corner ledge. Nest an open, rather shallow cup (or segment of cup in corner sites), made of pellets of mud intermingled with hay or straw, well-lined with feathers. 4–6 eggs, white, spotted variably with brownish-red. Usually a second brood, and often a third—sometimes in old nest, sometimes in fresh one, usually in same site.

25. Swift (above).
Swallow, male (below)

The House Martin and the Sand Martin

The House Martin Like the robin, this bird's pet-name has become its 'surname'; presumably it was once Martin Swallow, and thus distinguished from its cousin, then the 'chimney-swallow'. This bird is in fact 'a swallow' to a great many people, and '*the* swallow' to a great many town-dwellers, for owing to its different nesting requirements, the house martin has become the commoner of the two in built-up areas. It seems a bird eminently suitable for all grades of urban and suburban life, for its natural tendency is to live in communities, and there, beneath the sheltering eaves, its own dwellings may be detached, semi-detached or in continuous terraces. The analogy with human architecture could be carried further, for the martin also builds its residence with mineral matter, laid, like bricks, in single units of the material. Whether house martins merely get confused as to which nest is which, or whether the species has developed a commendable sense of neighbourliness unusual in colonial-nesting birds, is debatable; but the fact is that careful watching will reveal that more than two birds may be feeding the young in one nest. Once, at the beginning of October, when all the local house martins were assumed to have gone, a single nest was found still containing young—and no fewer than five mature birds were discovered to be shuttling to and fro with food.

The house martin's almost invariable choice of site for its nest on a building, a perpendicular wall with some projecting shelter (normally the eaves) above, gives some clue as to its ancestral nesting-site —a rock or cliff-face with projecting ledges or an overhang. A few such natural sites are still used, but in view of their comparative scarcity, the house martin, as the swallow, must have increased greatly with the advent of man the house-builder.

The Sand Martin This, the smallest of our three swallows, is usually the first to arrive, often before the end of March. All three species are attracted to the vicinity of water for feeding purposes, but as the sand martin's nesting-requirements—cliffs or banks of sand or earth—are frequently associated with water, one tends to think of it as the most water-haunting of the three. Just as the swallow and house martin have thrived with the multiplication of nesting-sites produced by man's building activities, so, less directly, has the sand martin. The digging of the raw materials for brick and concrete have made available the earth-faces of innumerable clay and gravel-pits, and these, wherever the softer layers prove penetrable, are readily colonised. Other fairly natural sites created by man can be found in railway cuttings through suitable soils, including soft chalk, or in the thick mortar between the stones of medieval masonry; more purely artificial sites, relieving the bird of the labour of tunnelling, are provided by drainage pipes in retaining walls in sites varying from riverside gardens to railway stations well away from water. It seems strange that of all the British species of perching-birds, this, one of the most aerial in habits, and not apparently endowed with highly specialised tools for the job, should have become the only excavator of tunnels in the earth.

Notes on The House Martin

HAUNTS   Provided that there is some open country within reach, almost any aggregation of buildings from isolated farm to suburbs of large cities.

APPEARANCE   A black and white bird, lacking swallow's long tail streamers and coloured breast, and slightly smaller, but most prominent feature is white rump. Feet white-feathered, including toes.

VOICE   Call, frequently uttered when on feeding or mud-gathering flights, a short 'chup' or 'churp'. Not such an obvious songster as the swallow, but occasionally sings snatches of thin twittering.

FOOD   Very much as for swallow, but tends to explore much higher in the air — feeding parties sometimes almost beyond unaided vision, and only detected by flight-calls.

NESTING   Nest built up of pellets of mud mixed with little fibrous binding material; courses of an inch or so built at a time, and allowed to harden before next is added. Final form an elongated cup against wall, with small top-opening beneath sheltering overhang; feather-lined. 4–5 glossy white eggs.

Notes on The Sand Martin

HAUNTS   On migration and passage frequently congregates in large flocks over water. Breeding haunts restricted by specialised requirements, but usually present whenever latter are available, from earthy sea-cliff to inland gravel pit or river-bank.

APPEARANCE   Swallow-like in both form and feeding habits, but much smaller and, quite appropriately, of an earthy-brown colour above; underside white, with conspicuous brown band across breast; tail only slightly forked.

VOICE   Normal call a harsh twitter, more grating and vibrant than that of house martin; song merely a more rapid elaboration of call. When alarmed (particularly at nesting-site) most frequent call is staccato 'trit-trit'.

FOOD   Entirely insects taken on wing; possibly, from usual proximity to water, aquatic insects in higher proportion than in other two swallows—though all three species may on occasion be feeding over water together.

NESTING   Burrow excavated in firm sand, soft marl or similar substances by both pecking and scratching; entrance hole usually a horizontally flattened oval; tunnel may penetrate from one to three feet, with widened nesting-chamber at end; little actual nest-building—chamber lined with few straws and feathers. 4–5 white, almost transparent shells, lacking gloss of those of house martin.

26. Sand Martin (middle and top two birds in flight). House Martin (below and lowest bird in flight)

The Kingfisher

Although this is surely one of the most conspicuous of British birds, so much so that it looks almost too exotic and jewel-like to be a native, it is surprising to discover how many people, even in suitable areas where they are not uncommon, confess that they have never seen a live specimen. Not a hundred yards from where this is being written is a narrow, steep-banked chalk-stream, where seven different kingfishers were known to have been present, usually singly, between late June and September; yet a resident whose paddock runs down to the stream has yet to see his first specimen. Even anglers who haunt known kingfisher sites from mid-June to mid-March may fail to catch a glimpse of the fleeting arrow of emerald, cobalt and orange, even though scores of opportunities must have been available in an average season.

The explanation for this blind spot in the powers of observation of otherwise observant people is that, more often than not, the opportunity for a satisfactory view may only exist for a fraction of a second. It is therefore essential to know when to look and where to look. The kingfisher is very prone to giving audible warning of approach—a shrill piping not unlike a louder version of the dunnock's call. Once this is learnt kingfisher spotting becomes easy, for one does not have to scan the whole sky but merely the surface of the water. It is possibly this flight close to the water which enables the kingfisher to pass by unnoticed; it is true that swallows are obvious enough when they are skimming just as close to the water, but their continual changing of course and visible wing-movements attract attention. The kingfisher's usual arrow-straight flight, and the illusion that it is moving without wing-beats, simply does not look bird-like.

Normally the kingfisher is sufficiently mobile and adaptable to survive a hard winter; if ponds or lakes freeze it will move to still flowing rivers; should these freeze, it can move to swifter rivers, or even to the sea shore. But in exceptional winters, such as that of 1962–63, almost all of these alternatives became inaccessible for fishing purposes, and judging by the lack of breeding records from many English counties in the following nesting-season, and the absence of sight records of even single birds in their old haunts, it seems that the kingfisher, although for different reasons, was as severely reduced in numbers as the wren. In totally different weather conditions the kingfisher can also show adaptability in altering its ways to suit different circumstances. It normally watches, and finally dives, for fish from some perch overhanging the water, but when a prolonged drought once caused the margin of a lake to recede until only dried mud lay beneath any available perch, the kingfishers did not leave, but fished like miniature ospreys—hovering over the water for the preliminary reconnaissance, then diving.

Notes on The Kingfisher

HAUNTS   For breeding needs water (not too swiftly flowing) for fishing, and banks in which to nest—requirements available at variety of fresh-water sites—rivers, streams, canals, large ponds (such as flooded gravel-pits), and lakes. In winter may frequent almost any waters where small fish and aquatic insects plentiful, from mere flooded ditches to brackish estuaries and salt coastal waters.

APPEARANCE   Most of upper surface iridescent bluish or greenish, varying from cobalt to almost emerald according to incidence of light; underparts rich chestnut-orange, and broad patch of same colour behind eye; conspicuous white on throat and sides of nape. Proportionately large head and beak, effect exaggerated by stumpy tail.

VOICE   Normal piping call already described. During mating season (and sometimes in chases in autumn) definite trilling song produced by acceleration of call-notes, delivered on wing or from perch.

FOOD   In addition to small fish (minnows, sticklebacks and fry of larger species), both larvae and adults of aquatic insects eaten.

NESTING   Deep tunnel with terminal nesting-chamber excavated in bank. No true nesting material, but regurgitated fish-bones accumulate to form nest-like mass beneath eggs or nestlings. Usually 6 eggs of glossy transparent white. Noise from young in burrow when parent enters with food a rapid mechanical twitter, reminiscent of old-fashioned horse mowing-machine at work.

27. Kingfisher

The Green Woodpecker

This, the largest of our three woodpeckers, differs from the others not only in size, but also in plumage, voice and habits. From its distinctive laughing call it has many country names, such as 'yaffle'; in some districts it is also the 'rain-bird', and the calls, loudest and most frequently uttered during mild April weather, are taken as 'boding rain'. Its most un-woodpeckerlike habit is that of feeding on the ground, and probably this source may provide the major part of its diet, for not only does it frequent drier ground in search of ants throughout the summer, but it may also be seen probing in damp lawns and pastures at other seasons, eating both earthworms and leatherjackets.

If blackbirds or starlings approach too closely on such occasions, a fascinating threat-display may sometimes be observed; the woodpecker stiffens in an upright position, elongates its neck to an extraordinary extent, bill pointing upwards, and slowly moves its head from side to side. The somewhat fearsome, snakelike performance, and the sinister appearance of the slightly puffed-out black moustaches, seem quite effective in warning-off possible competitors without the need for any more direct action. (It is interesting to note that a kingfisher reacts to the indignity of being held in the hand by a similar intimidating performance.) The green colour which gives this bird its name is most noticeable on such birds on the ground at close quarters; in flight the bright yellow of the rump is what catches the eye.

Since the green woodpecker's alternative mode of feeding makes it less dependent upon trees, it is the species most likely to be seen in prolonged flight when disturbed from the ground in open country; it thus affords the best opportunities for noting typical woodpecker flight—a few wing-beats upward, followed by a shallower plunge downward with closed wings, producing progress in a series of bouncing undulations.

In many areas there has been a marked decline in numbers of this species, once the commonest woodpecker in England (it was always scarcer to the northward, occurring sparingly in southern Scotland, and not at all in Ireland). It may be that its ground-feeding habits had become such an established part of its dietary routine that it could not obtain sufficient food during the long period of snow-cover in the winter of 1962–63. (It is far less likely to accept the hospitality of the bird-table than the pied woodpecker, although in some previous snowy winters, one would come regularly to peck at apples placed on the ground.) Another possibility, in view of the source of much of its food, is that through ants, leatherjackets and earthworms it may have accumulated lethal doses of the insidious farm and garden insecticides of modern times.

Notes on The Green Woodpecker

HAUNTS   Not so restricted to woodland as other woodpeckers—commons, gardens, parks and hedged meadows equally popular provided that some large trees are available.

APPEARANCE   At rest crimson crown and greenish plumage most obvious features; in flight larger size and yellow rump distinguish it from other woodpeckers. Sexes almost alike, but in male black 'moustache' bordered with crimson. Young have duller, more streaky red caps, breasts (unmarked in adults) speckled heavily, and pale tips to feathers giving mottled effect to greenish back-plumage.

VOICE   Cannot be put into words, but laughing quality unique among British bird sounds (excepting whinny of little grebe); laughing phrase usually begins loudly and fairly slowly, but rapidly gets faster, at the same time diminishing in both pitch and volume. A much slower, more subdued version may be heard at close range in spring. This laugh is true song and, unlike other two species, the green woodpecker has not developed drumming as a substitute. Call, frequently emitted in flight or when alarmed, a sharp 'twit-twit'.

FOOD   Insect grubs, from both wood-boring and ground; ants, both adults and 'eggs' (pupae); worms and millipedes; occasionally seeds or nuts.

NESTING   In specially excavated holes in tree-trunks; entrance-hole (about size of tennis-ball) continues horizontally inwards for few inches, then descends almost at right-angles to end in wider oval chamber, often more than a foot below entrance. No nesting-material, apart from wood-chippings. Eggs 5–7, pure white. (Nest-holes on completion often seized by starlings, and noisy squabbles in attempts to evict squatter ensue.)

28.   Green Woodpecker, male

The Pied Woodpecker and the Barred Woodpecker

The Pied Woodpecker   This name is deliberately chosen as preferable to 'greater spotted' wood-pecker, for while it is undeniable that it is the larger of our two black and white woodpeckers, the two contrasting colours are distributed in large patches rather than spots. Although living up to its name as a borer and excavator of timber in search of insect food, its fondness for nuts and other nutritious seeds, as a subsidiary diet, has probably led to its becoming a bird-table feeder in areas where there are sufficient large trees to serve as stepping-stones from woodland to garden. In order to split hard-shelled seeds—and it can deal with plumstones and peachstones as well as hazel-nuts—one foot is used as a clamp holding the nut against the perch, and the shell is opened by a series of rapid hammer-blows from the strong bill. The result is usually a neat splitting, rather than smashing. It will also readily take meaty or fatty scraps from the bird-table.

Another less desirable habit in woodland—that of excavating in search of young birds in nest-holes—has also been evident in garden-visiting pied woodpeckers, and many a tit-box has had its entrance enlarged and its contents eaten. Even a nest-box cast in concrete to foil such robberies has been known to have had the entrance considerably enlarged, a testimony both to the hardness of the bill and the power of the muscles behind it. But in spite of such depredations, this woodlander is welcomed as an exotic adornment to any bird-table, and its clinking call, drumming song and dipping flight are familiar contributions to woodland sounds and sights.

With the recent decline in numbers of the green woodpecker, the pied is now the most widespead and plentiful British woodpecker. It was never scarce, and the apparently recently-acquired bird-table habit, and the great increase in the provision of such sources of easy food (and of interested observers who watch them), have probably resulted in its being a bird more often seen than formerly, rather than a more plentiful bird; although no doubt such feeding has helped to tide the species over bad winters. But certainly it has spread and increased within the last half century, for it has succeeded in re-colonising Scotland, from which it had disappeared about a hundred years ago. It is quite at home in coniferous woods, provided that mature timber is present, and there pine-seeds, hacked out from the cones, are an important item of diet. It is absent as a breeding species from Ireland.

The Barred Woodpecker   Here again it has been thought logical to call the lesser of the two black and white woodpeckers by a name which accords with its appearance, for it is obviously barred, with no suggestion of spots. Two facts which make it seem rarer than it is (though it is by far the least plentiful of our three woodpeckers) are its small size—about that of a sparrow—and its habit of frequenting the higher reaches of large trees. Once its spring call—a high, clear 'pee-pee-pee', often repeated in long series—is known, it will often be detected by ear rather than eye; but often the singer is well out on a high twig, and may be more easy to spot than a drumming pied woodpecker.

This species also drums, but the sound is so similar to that of the other species that it is useless as a means of identification; it is proportionately quieter, but the same effect could be produced by a more distant pied woodpecker. At the first flight from the nesting-hole families may be seen frequenting lower trees than usual; on the occasion of one such dispersal one parent and three young were seen at close range on a small apple tree, and the 'pee-pee' call mixed with some 'chik-chik' notes was finally traced to the other parent actually perched on the telegraph wires across the road; the cause of its agitation was a fourth youngster spiralling up the telegraph post.

Notes on The Pied Woodpecker

HAUNTS Woodland, both deciduous and coniferous, if some mature timber present.

APPEARANCE Approximately size of starling, but stouter build and shorter tail; pied effect most noticeable on black back with broad white shoulder-patches, also on head, with black crown, white cheeks, and on white-barred quill-feathers. Other most striking feature is bright crimson present on lower belly and under tail of both male and female, and additional bar of the same colour between the crown and nape of the male, while juveniles, though lacking crimson underparts, are capped with this colour.

VOICE Call a metallic 'clink-clink'. Mechanical performance of drumming on resonant wood (sometimes metal) replaces spring song.

FOOD See main text.

NESTING Nesting-hole excavated in solid wood, usually fairly high in main trunk; entrance tunnelled inwards for some inches, then enlarged chamber formed downwards. Although same tree is often used, a new hole is usually made each year. 4–6 glossy white eggs laid on wood-chippings.

Notes on The Barred Woodpecker

HAUNTS Open woods, well-timbered parks and gardens, orchards, but, unlike larger species, not conifers. Rarer northwards—not occurring in Scotland.

APPEARANCE Apart from much smaller size, black and white pattern is quite distinct from that of pied, as wings and lower back completely barred. Both male and female also lack red beneath tail, but male has crimson crown, and both male and female juveniles have smaller traces of red in same position.

VOICE Has fainter edition of pied's clinking call. Since 'pee-pee-pee' call is mainly restricted to spring, it must be regarded as song, though presumably drumming also serves this purpose.

FOOD More entirely insectivorous than pied.

NESTING Nest hole always excavated in soft, partially rotten wood, sometimes quite low in dead stump, but may be very high in dead limb. Both nesting-chamber and eggs like those of pied, but proportionately smaller.

29. Pied Woodpecker, male (above).
Barred Woodpecker, male (below)

The Cuckoo

The cuckoo for many people is still, as it was for Wordsworth, a 'wandering voice' rather than a bird to be recognised when seen. 'The first cuckoo of the year has been heard in Blankshire' is the usual form of the evidence accepted as a news item by some local and even national newspapers—and the dates tend to become more incredible each year. To the conscientious recorder, therefore, the sight of the first cuckoo is all-important. This general concentration of interest upon the voice alone—common to both countryman and town-dweller—is all the more puzzling because excited sexual and territorial chases, often involving several birds, are common occurrences soon after arrival. The latter is normally from the beginning of April onwards. In most species of summer migrants (as is obvious in the easily identified cock blackcap) the male arrives well ahead of the female, in order to claim and establish a breeding-territory. This is unnecessary in the case of the cuckoo, since it is the female which is the chooser and holder of territory; thus not infrequently the first birds of both sexes may be seen on the same day. Since the far-carrying voice of the male is what usually alerts the observer, it is less often possible to encounter a bubbling female as the first cuckoo of the year—but when by chance this does occur, it is a peculiarly satisfying experience.

When perched the cuckoo gives an impression of precarious balance, as if the feet, with two toes in front and two behind, were not so efficient in ensuring a firm grip as in the arrangement common to true perching birds; this apparent instability becomes even more noticeable when the whole body wobbles at the tail-wag which accompanies each 'coo-coo' emitted.

The cuckoo's unique distinction among British birds is that of being our only brood-parasite, using other species both for the incubation of its eggs and the rearing of its offspring. The list of species used as foster-parents is extensive, but in each appropriate type of country there seems to be a favourite dupe—meadow pipit on mountain and moorland; dunnock in woodland, gardens and hedgerows; reed warbler in watery sites; and pied wagtail in man-made surroundings.

The most fascinating aspect of the cuckoo's migratory habits is the fact that the old birds, which had arrived from Africa in spring, depart on the return journey usually before the end of July, at a date when many of their offspring are still being fed in the foster-parent's nest. The young of the year may not depart until the middle of September; they must therefore make their first trip to Africa by purely instinctive navigational powers, without the benefit of experienced adults.

Notes on The Cuckoo

HAUNTS Widespread and various—in accordance with habitat favoured by species normally victimised.

APPEARANCE At rest, from rear, colour might suggest very slim pigeon—it is in fact about as long as stock dove, but more than half length is occupied by tail; from side or front-view barring of breast suggests sparrowhawk; sexes very similar, but male tends to bluer on back, and has unbarred grey on throat and upper breast. Juvenile browner, with pale edges to feathers giving scaly effect, and conspicuous white patch on nape. In flight much like cock sparrowhawk until pointed wings and graduated white-tipped tail are noted; but resemblance sufficient to make domestic fowl dash for cover when cuckoo flies low overhead.

VOICE Apart from 'coo-coo' (which from immediately beneath can sound more like 'phoo-phoo'), and stuttering versions of the same song, male often emits preliminary guttural gurgle (with little carrying power) before typical call; female's call a bubbling sound, sometimes almost a bubbling whistle.

FOOD Almost entirely insects, especially caterpillars; latter include hairy types such as those of tiger-moth (woolly bears) and tortoiseshell butterfly.

NESTING Egg removed by female from fosterer's nest (and usually eaten) and own egg laid directly into nest. One female has area in which she watches activities of potential dupes; one species usually adhered to as chosen fosterer. Eggs extremely variable, those of dunnock and pied wagtail-parasites being usually greyish and spotted, and those of pipit parasites more frequently brownish or reddish. Young or unhatched eggs lifted in hollow of back of newly-hatched cuckoo and ejected from nest.

30. Cuckoo, male

The Tawny Owl

This is the owl frequently heard, but less often seen, a reversal of the status of the barn owl; but since it is both a much more plentiful and a more vocal species than the latter, the chances of hearing a tawny owl are infinitely greater than those of seeing a barn owl. The tawny, wood, or brown owl is strictly nocturnal, rarely venturing out by daylight even when it has young to feed, and the best chances of seeing it by day probably occur when one is disturbed from its sleeping-roost by a walker off the beaten track in woodland; both dense plantations of conifers and the ivy clumps on small trees are favourite roosting-sites; in town gardens, parks and cemeteries the darkness afforded by yews is likewise sought during hours of daylight. The chance discovery of such a lodger by some foraging tit or wren may lead to the sounding of a general alarm which will be taken up by every other tit, wren, dunnock, chaffinch and blackbird in the neighbourhood, and the excited 'mobbing' of the owl which follows will often force it to take flight in broad daylight, pursued by its tormentors.

But although the familiar call may be heard through the night-traffic in the centres of large towns and cities, the tawny owl is essentially a woodland bird, feeding on woodmice, shrews and beetles on the ground, and taking the occasional roosting bird from a bush. In suitable circumstances, birds easily caught may form a substantial part of the diet in autumn and winter, the most frequent example being the regular nightly feeding on starlings if a roost of these birds happens to form conveniently in a tawny owl's feeding-territory. For many weeks at one such site, where the owl spent the day in a Scots pine and the starlings came each evening to the hawthorn-scrub just below, the evidence of the regurgitated pellets—feathers, bones and often complete skulls or feet—left no doubt as to the suitability of the arrangement from the owl's point of view. Here, on one moonlight night, the hunter was seen in the act of flying around a dense thorn seething with starlings clambering inwards like ants; at times the owl's wing actually brushed against the twigs audibly, but it is difficult to say whether this was just an accidental contact while hovering for a pounce, or a deliberate attempt to beat a victim out into reach. Unfortunately, at this point the observer was himself observed, and the owl flew off.

Young tawny owls, still fluffy, may frequently be found out of the nest, often on the ground, long before they are able to fly; two such, little more than half grown, were once found huddled in the cavity between the buttress-roots of a beech, but the remains of a very young rabbit beneath them suggested that they were not in need of care, and subsequent visits proved that they were thriving and by no means abandoned. Kind-hearted (or acquisitive) 'rescues' of such owlets, even if they are reared successfully, can have only two outcomes—a life in captivity, or a release at maturity into a wild life for which they have not served the very necessary long apprenticeship with their parents; and neither is desirable.

Notes on The Tawny Owl

HAUNTS   Woodland, deciduous or coniferous, or parks and gardens with mature trees.

APPEARANCE   Lack of ear-tufts, stouter body and dark eyes distinguish this from only other brown owl likely to be seen perching in woodland. Colour rich warm brown, mottled darker, on back, with buffer shoulder-patch; breast paler, with dark streaks. (But colour variable, some individuals almost as red as cock pheasant, some as pale as hen pheasant.) In flight, long, rounded wings and very large head noticeable; if seen head-on, round (as opposed to heart-shaped) facial disc separates this from barn owl when colour not plainly seen.

VOICE   Common call is a loud, repeated 'kewik'. Song of male is long-drawn out, undulating hoot so easily imitated by blowing into hollow cupped hands. Traditional 'too-wit-too-woo' is either duet between female calling 'kewick' and male answering 'too-woo', or frequently combination of preliminary call followed by hooting from one bird.

FOOD   Small mammals—mice, voles, shrews, moles; larger insects, chiefly beetles; and small birds or young of larger species.

NESTING   In hollow of tree or (mainly in evergreens) on foundation of old nest of crow or pigeon. In dense conifer plantations not infrequently on ground beneath heaps of branches left from trimming stems. No nesting material added and, unlike barn owl, does not cast up pellets in nest-hole. Eggs pure white of a roundish oval shape (no big or little end), usually 2, followed by further 2 at intervals of some days.

31. Tawny Owl

The Barn Owl

Although by no means as plentiful as the tawny owl, the barn owl is probably seen far more often than the commoner species. This is not only because of its preference for human haunts—from farm barns to village belfries—for roosting and nesting, but also on account of its feeding habits. For it quarters the open fields, rather than woodland, in search of prey and, particularly in late winter, may often begin its forays in the dim daylight of the afternoon. It is even more likely to be seen in daylight during the evenings throughout May and June, when the protracted business of rearing young is in full swing. Then, once the location of the feeding-beat has been discovered, the hunter (or hunters, since a pair, recognisably different in plumage, will be involved) can be watched at leisure.

The hunting technique is fairly constant: a leisurely, buoyant flight only a few feet above the herbage, now and again billowing up to twenty feet or so, as if to gain impetus for the next run; occasional hesitant wavering, sometimes developing into momentary winnowing hovers; an inclination to follow the field boundaries, whether hedges, walls or railway embankments; and the final moment when sight takes over from hearing in the location of the prey and there is a rapid shoot downward with legs to the fore and with wings extended but cupped forward. Whether the latter position, which always seems to accompany the kill, is merely an essential manoeuvre for abrupt braking, or whether it may muffle any attempt at escape on the part of the prey, is uncertain. Another interesting point, which may be clearly observed on such daylight patrols, is that the short tail is fanned out to form a continuous flying surface with the wings, and is apparently little used as a rudder; the long legs, however, stretched out behind, are continually in motion, and obviously serve as steerage organs.

On such occasions one can get close-up views of the delicately patterned colour of the upper surface—basically a pale golden buff, stippled with minute points of grey, black and white. The female usually has darker stippling, and this is often heavy enough to suggest a lavender-grey bloom dusted over the underlying buff. But the most striking view of all is that of a barn owl approaching the observer at eye-level; then the large head completely blots out the comparatively small body, and all one sees is the unique heart-shaped face—pure white, black-eyed and outlined with a ridge of stiff dark feathers—suspended between two long wings.

The name 'white owl' is appropriate only when this bird is seen at dusk (or floodlit in the beam of the motorist's headlamps), for then only its pure white underparts show up. At such times, in the face-to-face view already mentioned, the eerie apparition can be that of a disembodied face silently floating towards one. These ghostly appearances, combined with the hair-raising screech and its churchyard associations, have all tended to give this useful parishioner an undeservedly sinister reputation.

Notes on The Barn Owl

HAUNTS   May occur anywhere, in town or country, where combination of dark, accessible lodging (building or hollow tree) and open hunting ground is available.

APPEARANCE   At rest, most striking feature is heart-shaped white face, unlike that of any other species; upright stance; long, white-feathered legs; breast apparently pure white, but may be slightly spotted. In flight, general impression of ghostly whiteness at night or in dusk; by day silvery-white underparts, yellowish upper parts, and hunting behaviour—and unforgettable face.

VOICE   This is the screech owl, and there is little more that can be said, except that the screech is long-drawn-out, blood-curdling, and often emitted in flight.

FOOD   Mainly small mammals—mice, voles and shrews; not infrequently birds, particularly house sparrows and starlings. Pellet analysis illustrates variability in size of meals, dependent on factors such as weather and scarcity or abundance of prey—thus a good meal might be six wood-mice, or four shrews and two field-voles, while a poor night's hunting might be represented by only two small mammals of this size.

NESTING   No nest made; pure white eggs laid in sites such as on floor or wall-ledge in dark corner of barn-loft, or on wood-debris in cavernous tree; pellets or food-castings soon accumulate, so that ultimately young may appear to be on a 'nest' of this material. Size of family, as in most owls, related to food supply; basic clutch of 2 eggs, but often augmented by similar clutches at intervals of about a week; thus nests can be found with 'staggered' contents—often 2 eggs, two young still in fluffy white down, and the first-born pair half-fledged.

32. Barn Owl

The Kestrel

With the noble peregrine a diminishing frequenter of rugged cliffs and mountains, the nimble merlin an inhabitant of open moorland, and the hobby an uncommon summer migrant, the only British falcon widely seen and known is the one most un-falconlike in behaviour, the kestrel. Since it obtains most of its prey, not after a high-speed chase and headlong stoop, but by a sudden plunge after a leisurely scanning of the ground from a series of winnowing surveys from high above, punctuated by frequent static hovers when some slight movement on the ground demands closer scrutiny, its mode of hunting attracts attention. Furthermore, although it can flourish in coastal or mountain haunts as remote as those of the peregrine, it is also equally at home over farmland or town.

Most farmers realize its value as a mouser, and since it is less prone to hunt in woodland it has never been persecuted by gamekeepers to the same extent as the sparrowhawk. Therefore, until quite recently, not only its conspicuous aerial habits, but also its abundance in total numbers, made it an almost everyday bird for most countrymen and not a few townsmen. Within the last three or four years there has been an alarming decline in kestrel population, almost certainly attributable to the use of poisonous pesticides. It was notable that when this decrease was first evident over the mainly arable (or horticultural) south-eastern half of England, kestrels were still as common as formerly in coastal areas of the west and south-west, where mice and beetles were as yet untainted with organic chlorine poisons.

The kestrel must surely be the origin of the expression 'eyes like a hawk' as a simile for keenness of vision. To see a kestrel hovering over a hundred feet high above a grassfield, then plummet down to a kill with extended foot—and then, as the prize is taken to a nearby fence-post, to discover through binoculars that the prey was only a beetle about half-an-inch in diameter, although somewhat of an anti-climax to the excitement of the proceedings, is nevertheless a revelation of the telescopic powers of vision possessed by this bird.

The old names of 'wind-hover' and 'stand-gale' for this falcon suggest an awareness of the actual mechanics of its hovering technique; although this is an over-simplification of what actually occurs, basically 'standing still' in the air is achieved by regulating the speed of flight to match exactly the speed of the wind which it faces. Presumably a kestrel would be unable to hover in a complete calm; presumably also, the air is never in this motionless state, so the difficulty never arises.

Although the kestrel is usually seen in typical hunting flight—alternately flapping for a few beats and then gliding or hovering—it may, particularly in late summer or early autumn, sometimes be observed high and flying on a direct course, when it may be mistaken for a peregrine. It is known that some young kestrels move southward at the approach of their first winter, and since such stray birds are most frequently observed flying southwards (not infrequently in association with swallows) these pseudo-peregrines are assumed to be birds in this category. An interesting point which ringing of young kestrels, and subsequent recoveries, has revealed, is that out of one brood, one bird may be such a winter emigrant, moving some hundreds of miles to the south, while another may still be within a few miles of its home during its first winter.

Notes on The Kestrel

HAUNTS Almost any type of country with open hunting-ground—arable, parkland, rugged coast or hills, marshes, even towns or cities with large open spaces; but some prominence, whether tree, crag or high building, desirable for roosting and nesting.

APPEARANCE In flight identifiable by manner of prospecting and feeding, for no other British hawk (or bird of any other British species) habitually feeds by hovering over open country. Male has contrasting plumage of almost pigeon-grey and chestnut—grey on head, rump and tail, latter with broad black band with narrow rim of white near tip; remainder of back and upper wing chestnut spotted with black; flight quills blackish; underparts paler reddish-buff, with dark vertical streaks. Female and young lack grey, but apart from this plumage of similar pattern, but duller. But since it takes three years for young male to acquire fully adult plumage, intermediate stages of plumage, particularly with regard to amount of grey, can be seen.

VOICE Usually a silent bird except when mating or feeding young, when an excited, very loud and shrill 'klee-klee-klee' call is used.

FOOD Ground-mammals—mice, voles, shrews, moles, rats and sometimes very young rabbits; insects, mainly larger species such as cockchafer, dung-beetle and grasshopper; birds taken usually small ground-feeding species such as sparrows and finches, struck as they feed or immediately as they rise, not captured in full flight. Mammals and insects usually carried to perch for consumption, but birds may be plucked on ground.

NESTING No nest is built, but eggs are laid on ledge on crag or building, or in hollow of tree, or in wooded areas, frequently on old nests of crow or magpie. Pellets of indigestible food remains are cast up and accumulate in 'nest'. Usually 4–5 eggs, of whitish ground-colour heavily blotched with deep reddish-brown—usually little of ground-colour visible.

33. Kestrel, male

The Moorhen and the Mallard

The Moorhen This bird's name dates back to the days when a moor was any type of waste-land unsuitable for cultivation; thus on some soils the 'moors' would be ill-drained land, semi-marsh with more or less permanent pools, and these would be the haunts of the moorhen. The alternative name, water-hen, is nowadays more apt, but the quantity of water needed to form the basis of a moorhen's territory may be surprisingly small; a little duckpond on a village green, an even smaller pool in dense woodland, or a downland dewpond, in each case several miles from any other water, are all actual examples of the minimal requirements which will suffice for one pair of birds. These examples, together with the alacrity with which new artificial pools (near suitable cover) are tenanted, suggests that there is always a surplus population prospecting for new homes. The isolated breeding-sites mentioned must surely have first been espied from the air, yet the moorhen is seldom seen in sustained flight. Like others of the rail family—coot, corncrake and water rail—the moorhen probably performs its migratory movements by night. Thus it has been noted, at sites such as old gravel-pits used as refuse-dumps, or the old-fashioned sewage-farm, both very attractive as winter-haunts for large moorhen assemblies, that numbers may increase greatly between one dusk and the ensuing dawn.

Of all the rails the moorhen is the least specialised and therefore the most versatile; its toes have only developed slight edging membrane as an aid to swimming, yet it swims as freely as the lobe-footed coot; its extremely long toes are as efficient for walking on oozy mud as those of the water rail; it can elongate its body and thread its way through dense vegetation as rapidly and as rat-like as either water rail or corncrake; and—an achievement which sets it apart—it can exploit higher levels of vegetation, for not only may it sometimes roost and nest high in a hawthorn hedge, but also it may walk along the top of the same hedge to feed on haws.

The Mallard This species was once known as 'the wild duck' with no further qualification, and the term 'mallard' was reserved for the drake bird. It is our commonest species of duck, and though wary in the wild in the breeding-season, or in wildfowling districts in winter, wildness is not its outstanding characteristic, for when it senses safe surroundings it rapidly becomes tame. Thus the hand-fed birds which frequent many urban pools in winter may, not many weeks previously, have been genuinely wild, both in the free and nervous sense of that word. Since among animals trust, like fear, seems an infectious emotion, no doubt the presence of already tame ornamental species helps the rapid adjustment in such conditions.

The mallard is a typical 'dabbling' duck, feeding either from the surface or just below without diving, and in shallow water frequently 'up-ending' to feed from the bottom; but it can also feed on dry land and it is a regular gleaner of stubbles, often by night, and often many miles from water. Its inclination to nocturnal activities accounts for the fact that a great part of the day seems to be spent, particularly if a sanctuary such as an islet is available, in sleeping, preening or sun-bathing. It is a powerful flier, and in winter visitors from northern and eastern Europe augment our resident population. It is also the ancestor of most breeds of domestic ducks, and where the latter have access to waters frequented by mallard (and *vice versa*) interbreeding often occurs.

Notes on The Moorhen

HAUNTS
Still or slow-flowing fresh water, with reedy or bushy ground-cover available, together with more open tracts of grass and low herbage for extensive foraging.

APPEARANCE
On water looks mainly blackish (actually slatey-grey with browner wings), with slanting white line across flanks just below wing, bright red on shield on forehead extending to base of bill, contrasting with yellow of latter, and jerky tail-movement exposing white under tail. On land, long-toed yellowish-green feet, with red and yellow 'garter' above so-called 'knee', a very conspicuous feature.

VOICE
A harsh, purring croak—'purruck'; also a clicking call, sometimes single, but in excitement becoming a continuous 'kik-kik-kik.'

FOOD
Mainly vegetable—seeds, shoots, duckweed, and berries. Some animal matter—earthworms, slugs, snails and insects.

NESTING
Nest a solid construction of reeds and rushes, with well-formed cup, usually at water-level among aquatic plants or in cover on ground at edge of water; but may build similar nest (usually on foundation such as old nest of wood pigeon) up to twenty feet high in tree. 8–12 eggs, stone-coloured with variable amount of purplish-brown and greyish blotching and spotting.

Notes on The Mallard

HAUNTS
Widespread and varied, with no marked preference for any one type or size of water—very similar to moorhen in variable, but always water-based, range of haunts. Large flocks after breeding, later augmented by winter-immigrants, prefer larger sheets of water—lakes, reservoirs, estuaries and coastal waters.

APPEARANCE
On water chief features of drake are glossy dark-green head, white collar, plum-coloured breast, finely patterned pale-grey back, and speculum (colour-patch on wing) iridescent purple-blue bordered on each side by black and white. Female brownish, but with same distinctive speculum. On land orange-red feet conspicuous. In flight wing-pattern surest means of separation from other wild duck of similar size.

VOICE
Well-known 'quack' is female's call; male utters more nasal and prolonged 'quek'. A contented, subdued chattering 'kek-kek-kek-kek-kek' common when feeding, but is also preliminary to alarmed take-off.

FOOD
Mainly vegetable—seeds (including grain, beechmast and acorns), duckweed, shoots and leaves of both land and water-plants; animal food includes earthworms, slugs, snails, insects, frogspawn, tadpoles and frogs.

NESTING
Ground-sites well hidden beneath reed-tussocks or undergowth; but in some districts crowns of pollard-willows much used. Chief feature of nest is abundance of speckled down, intermingled with dead leaves or grass; clutch often loosely concealed by down before incubation begins. 8–12 eggs, varying from greenish-blue to greenish-buff.

34. Moorhen (above).
Mallard, male (below)

The Wood Pigeon, the Stock Dove and the Turtle Dove

The Wood Pigeon   To a countryman one of the most striking features of bird-life in the parks of London is the sight of the wood pigeon as a fearless mixer with mankind, for in the country this is one of the most wary and unapproachable of birds. Since the country wood pigeon often associates with the smaller stock dove, it seems likely that the presence of the well-fed 'London pigeon' transmits a sense of security to this more unlikely candidate for citizenship. Anyone who has seen large winter flocks of wood pigeons must wonder (if he accepts the generally held belief that they are British-bred birds, unaugmented by foreign immigrants) where they have all come from, and why they are such an obviously successful species. Their nests neither conceal nor protect their eggs; their clutch is of two eggs only, and these, from their whiteness, are so conspicuous that they seem doomed to be found by the egg-thieving crow or jay. Pure white eggs are typical of birds which habitually nest in dark holes—owls, woodpeckers and kingfishers—and therefore need no nest-building skills. It is perhaps significant that many members of the pigeon family, including our stock dove and rock dove, are still in this category. This suggests that the wood pigeon has deviated from the ways of some distant ancestral hole-nester and has become only partially adapted in the matter of nest-construction, and totally unadapted with regard to egg-colour. Yet, in spite of these apparent drawbacks, wood pigeon population keeps at a remarkably high level. Three main factors contribute to this success: the wood pigeon has a long expectation of life, probably from ten to fifteen years; although it raises a small family, the breeding-season is protracted, and three broods are usual between April and December; and most helpful of all, the virtual absence of controlling predators, from large hawks to pine-martens.

The Stock Dove   Since this is a fairly large bird (though smaller than the wood pigeon), not infrequently nesting near dwellings, and in addition having a quite distinct pattern of cooing, it must lack qualities which attract general attention, for it tends to be overlooked. Even when recognised by farmers and gamekeepers as a separate species, and not just a 'small pigeon', it is often misleadingly referred to as a 'rock pigeon' or 'blue rock'. Certainly it is a much less plentiful species than the wood pigeon, but in some areas pure flocks of this species, often running into hundreds, may congregate on ploughed fields, fallows and stubbles.

The old adage about 'birds of a feather', with its implication that those in known bad company can be up to no good, is not very sound natural history. Thus from a mixed bag of 'pigeons' shot from a field of stooked wheat, while examination revealed the expected contents in the crops of the wood pigeons, the stock doves contained nothing but charlock-seed.

The Turtle Dove   This bird has all the appeal which the stock dove seems to lack; in the first place it is so obviously a dove, with all the connotations of peace and tranquillity connected with this name, and not a pigeon; it is also strikingly coloured, with a conspicuous fan-tail; it has the seasonal thrill of the returning migrant, and also a lazy, purring song which is the most soothing of summer sounds. Not for nothing did Solomon single it out by name among the heralds of summer—'The time of the singing of birds is come, and the voice of the turtle is heard in our land'.

Notes on The Wood Pigeon

HAUNTS   Open country, preferably both grassland and arable, with trees for cover and nesting; for latter purpose anything from dense coniferous woods to scrub and hedges.

APPEARANCE   Larger size and prominent white bar across wing separate from other bluish-grey wild pigeons. White neck-patch (hence 'ring dove') on adults only. Breast faintly iridescent shades of mauve, pink and brown. Tail mainly black, white-barred beneath.

VOICE   Notes usually uttered in series of five—'coo-coo-coo-coo-roo'—almost always ending, after a succession of such phrases, with a single note which sounds like the first one of another phrase.

FOOD   Almost entirely vegetable; apart from grain and clover, some staple items are acorns, beechmast, haws, ivy-berries, brassica crops, and buttercup corms.

NESTING   In trees and bushes at varying heights—may be only three feet in juniper or thorn scrub, but high in crowns of mature conifers. Nest may be mere platform of latticed twigs, or denser aggregation from repeated nestings on old base. 2 eggs, pure glossy white, almost even-ended.

Notes on The Stock Dove

HAUNTS   Often open woodland or timbered parks, but trees not essential for breeding.

APPEARANCE   Smaller and bluer than wood pigeon, with no white wing-bar or neck 'ring'. Two short black bars on blue of wing, though not extensive, conspicuous when bird is at rest.

VOICE   Cooing phrase of three notes—'oo-a-roo, oo-a-roo'—more rapid and slurred than wood pigeon's.

FOOD   Generally as for wood pigeon; but see main text.

NESTING   In any dark cavity—hollow trees, recesses in masonry, quarry or thatch, and in rabbit-burrows in treeless areas. No structure, but few straws and twigs may form lining. 2 eggs, smaller and less glossy white than pigeon's.

Notes on The Turtle Dove

HAUNTS   Open shrubby country, rather than true woodland—thorn-scrub, large gardens, parks, shrubberies and bushy commons.

APPEARANCE   At rest chief features, apart from small size compared with grey pigeons, are reddish brown, with blue-grey edging on wing, contrasting with dark flight-feathers of wing and tail; head and breast pigeon-like, but on neck, corresponding to wood pigeon's 'ring', a black-striped patch of pale grey. In flight long graduated tail forms white-rimmed fan.

VOICE   A deep, continuous purring, with very slight pauses between every phrase of three or four 'purrs'.

FOOD   Almost entirely vegetable, particularly seeds of weeds, especially fumitory.

NESTING   Nests in dense shrubs and trees—hawthorn, blackthorn, box, juniper. Nest a miniature version of wood pigeon's, of fine twigs and fibres. 2 eggs, glossy white.

35. Wood Pigeon (above).
Stock Dove (below, left).
Turtle Dove (below, right)

The Lapwing

This, perhaps the best-known British member of the wader group, is also in some ways an untypical representative of that fascinating family, both in appearance and habits. Its broad rounded wings bear little resemblance to the narrower, more pointed and angled wings of the typical wader in flight; and the flight itself is normally floppy and leisurely, again unwaderlike characteristics. It may also inhabit haunts such as dry arable or downland, instead of marshes and sea-shores; and its crested head gives it an appearance unique among British birds. But in other respects there is no mistaking the family to which it belongs—nesting habits, eggs, chicks; wild, musical calls as both songs and alarms; a conspicuous plumage-pattern in flight, and the formation of roving flocks immediately breeding is finished—all proclaim its affinities. Once breeding is over, where waterlogged furrows, flooded meadows or muddy estuaries offer opportunities, the lapwing will wade as freely as a redshank and, of course, may occupy marshy as well as dry sites for nesting.

Apart from the characteristic swoops and tumbles, which are so noticeable an accompaniment of the spring song, lapwings also display conspicuous aerial dexterity in their wandering autumn and winter flocks, and their long-extended line-abreast formations, rippling alternately black and white as the light strikes them, form and reform as if just for the enjoyment of disciplined flying manoeuvres.

The call is so well known that 'peewit' is about as generally used as lapwing as the name of this bird; the spelling 'pewit' may refer to a different interpretation of the call—certainly Tennyson used it as a rhyme for 'cruet'.

Although, except in conditions of severe frost, lapwings are usually to be seen in most localities throughout the whole year, the population is by no means static, except at nesting-time. Many British-bred birds move southward or westward to winter, perhaps only to south-west England or Eire, but often to France and Spain. Those still frequenting the old haunts may be winter-visitors from as far away as central or eastern Europe. (Two birds marked by the writer within a few fields of one another are good examples of this: one, ringed as a chick in May, turned up in the south-west of France in the following December; another, rescued from drowning after alighting on liquid sewage-sludge during winter, was found dead several years later, during the summer, on the borders of Poland and Czechoslovakia.) Weather-movements, possibly only to the unfrozen coast, are often resorted to, and departing or returning flocks sometimes seem to be just ahead of the weather conditions responsible for them.

In addition to the gaiety which the lapwing contributes to the rural scene, its presence is welcomed by the farmer for more practical reasons—it is a great consumer of wireworms and other soil pests.

Notes on The Lapwing

HAUNTS   At all times open country with very short vegetation, or ploughland. Most typical breeding-site now arable land, but also short turf of downs, tussocky marshes and damp moorland. After breeding, sites with similar feeding facilities—newly mown meadows, playing-fields, airfields and seashore.

APPEARANCE   Crested head and bold black and white plumage most distinctive features; black of back has greenish sheen—hence the 'green plover'; in spite of contrasting plumage, a well-spaced flock of motionless birds standing in open country can be remarkably inconspicuous.

VOICE   The 'pee-wit' call, usually uttered in flight, is basis of both spring song and alarm notes; often elaborated into 'pee-a-wit-wit-wit'; subdued warning or rallying-calls to chicks, usually uttered by distant standing parent, a long single note—'pee' without final 'wit'. (At very close quarters 'fee-it' is heard rather than traditional rendering.)

FOOD   Almost entirely animal matter—insects and their larvae, slugs, snails, earthworms and, on sea-shore, small crustaceans.

NESTING   Normally a scrape on bare ground, with mere vestiges of lining material such as dead grass; but in watery ground material may be sufficient to raise nest well above ground; when rising water threatens, this may be added to until almost as substantial as that of moorhen. Clutch typical of wader, 4 pear-shaped eggs closely fitted with points at centre; egg colour variable—from pale stone colour to dark or greenish-brown, mottled and spotted with black, but always inconspicuous whether on bare earth or grass. Chicks active as soon as dry after hatching, but freeze into immobility and invisibility at parent's alarm-call.

36. Lapwing